THE SECRETS OF SUPERSTARS

What Topnotch People Know and You Don't

AKWASI O. OFORI

The Secrets of Superstars © copyright 2024 by Akwasi O. Ofori. All rights reserved. No part of this book may be reproduced in any form whatsoever, by photography or xerography or by any other means, by broadcast or transmission, by translation into any kind of language, nor by recording electronically or otherwise, without permission in writing from the author, except by a reviewer, who may quote brief passages in critical articles or reviews.

Paperback ISBN: 979-8-9904106-7-1
Hardcover ISBN: 979-8-9904106-6-4
Ebook ISBN: 979-8-9904106-8-8

Book cover design by Jess LaGreca, Mayfly book design

Library of Congress Catalog Number: 2024908751
First Printing: 2024
Printed in the United States

For true success ask yourself these four questions:
Why? Why not? Why not me? Why not now?
James Allen

DEDICATION

To my dear wife Betty,
a true gem who never relinquishes her hold on hope.
Also, to my sister, Lizzie, the nurturer of hope.

CONTENTS

Introduction xv

Chapter One—Unrealized Potential 1
The Prize for Bad Judgments 1
Life's Conundrums 1
All People are Prone to Making Mistakes 3
Possibilities for Recovery 4
God's Master Plan for You 4
Individuals Uniquely Endowed 5
Factors that Affect Individual Development 6

**Chapter Two—Work Hard, Work Smart, Stay Focused
 and Succeed** 9
The Consequences of One's Work Ethic 9
The Human Quest for Success 10
Equip Yourself with the Appropriate Skill 11
The Shining Example of Jackie Robinson 13
Every Profession Equally Important 14
Training Can Make a Difference 16
Don't Discount Providence in Your Personal Development 17
Never Give Up Without a Fight 18
Building Your Idiosyncrasy Credits 19

**Chapter Three—Avoid Procrastination—
It Has Stalling Effects** 21
Procrastination, the Stonewall Effect 21
Procrastination: The Causes, the Sustaining Dynamics 22
The Result of Procrastination 23
The Advantages of Decisiveness 23
Ways to Stop Procrastination 24
The Right Time to Act 25

Chapter Four—Fear Has Crippling Effects 27
Fear, an Integral Part of Human Personality 27
Positive and Negative Fear 28
The Crippling Effects of Fear 29
God, Ever Present, Ever Helpful 31
Practical Steps to Overcoming Fear 33
From Fear to Boldness 34

Chapter Five—Stop Worrying, It's a Nuisance 37
A State of Worry 37
Reasons Why People Worry 38
The Leading Cause of Peoples' Worry 39
The Negative Effects of Worry 40
Reasons Why You Should Not Worry 42
Deal with Your Pattern of Worry 43
God's Providence Eases All Worry 44
Steps to Cut Down Worry 45
Where to Find Lasting Peace 46

Chapter Six—Enthusiasm Has Positive Effects 49
What Is Enthusiasm? 49
Personality Type and Enthusiasm 50
The Expressive Personality 51

The Driver Personality 52
The Amiable Personality 52
The Analytical Personality 53
The Role of Personality Type, and then Some 53
The Misery-Happiness Line 54
The Controlled Personality 55
Depression and Enthusiasm 56
Steps to Overcome Depression and Stay Enthusiastic 57

**Chapter Seven—Hold On To Undying Hope
it will Sustain You** 61
Wait and Hope 61
The Merits of Waiting 62
Waiting Bucks Today's Trend 63
Drawbacks to Impatience 64
The Irritation of Waiting 66
Waiting for the Right Moment 66
Waiting is a Show of Strength 69
Hold on to Undying Hope 70

Chapter Eight—Tactfulness Has Positive Benefits 73
Taking the Tactful Approach 73
When to Apply Tact 75
The Scope of Tactfulness 76
The Role of Tact in Communication 78
The Benefits of Being Tactful 80
The Appropriate Use of Tact 82

Chapter Nine—There is a Miracle in Giving 85
The Human Spirit of Showing Generosity 85
The Heart of Generosity 86

Different Ways of Showing Generosity 88
The Benefits of Acts of Kindness 89
The Obstacles to Generous Giving 91

Chapter Ten—Invigorate Your Life through Faith 93
Faith—an Essential Ingredient for Life 93
Why Faith is Important 94
Optimize Your Faith 96
The Faith to Blossom 97
The Next Leve 98
Obstacles to Faith 99

Chapter Eleven—There is Healing in Forgiving 101
Forgiveness is a Healing Balm 101
The Two-Fold Restorative Function of Forgiveness 102
Forgiveness Restores Broken Relationships 103
Forgiveness Restores Self-Worth 105
Forgiveness Restores a Healthy Self-Image 106
Why Forgiveness is Necessary 107

Chapter Twelve—The Secrets of Superstars 109
You Can Get Your Life on Track 109
You Can Still Be at Your Optimal Best 111
Change Your Belief System 111
Be a Person of Faith 112
Change Yourself, Change Your Circumstances 114
Forgive, Muster Courage and March On 115

Bibliography 117
About the Author 125

FOREWORD

This book is written for those who have underachieved in life from the viewpoint of a Christian leader. Hence, it is written with the Christian believer in view.

However, I am aware that not everybody believes in the Christian God. If you are such a person, you can still benefit greatly from this book because its lessons are universal.

My hope in writing this book is to help you as a reader to find answers to your shortfalls and reap the advantages of knowing your true self. Therefore, I will entreat you to read it cover to cover so that you can thoroughly digest the subject matter and apply it to enrich your life.

ACKNOWLEDGMENTS

Throughout my life, I have benefitted from the good counsel of many people. They kept me in crucial times when I tethered on the brink of failure. These timely counsels came on occasions when I seemed truly at the end of my rope.

Besides the good counsel from others, I have also, at different times in my life, received practical help from some people. These individuals are the real heroes and heroines who have made me who I am.

The first among these heroines is Betty, my wife, who has supported me in various ways. Whenever the going was tough, and I wanted to throw in the towel, she would urge me on. Then there is my sister, Lizzie, who nurtured me earlier in life and gave me the chance without which I would probably have remained irrelevant and trivial in life's journey.

Others would be Benefaa and Abena, my two daughters. These fast-growing young ladies give me a cause for living. Together, these people, through their perseverance and support, continually motivate me to write. A special mention should be made of Adwoa, my middle daughter, who passed away before this book was published. May her soul rest in peace.

My thanks also go to the editor, Mr. Alastair Tucker, and the publishers of this book. This expression of appreciation would not be complete without acknowledging the many authors whose works I consulted in writing this book.

These authors, whom I see as trailblazers, have trodden a path that has made it possible for some of us to find our way. In conclusion, I also want to show my gratitude to numerous others who helped me in diverse ways. May the Lord God bless all of you.

Akwasi O Ofori
Denver, Colorado

INTRODUCTION

I have stumbled on some secrets and have put them in this book, *The Secrets of Superstars*. It is written for you whose life has waned, leaving you feeling you have hit a wall. Most likely, you started life with high hopes, but now do not know what has become of all your desires and the drive to fulfill them. This development might have left you low on confidence.

As a result of your lack of confidence, you might wrongly assume that you cannot stem the mediocre lifestyle and the poor results you see. Thus, you are often tempted to throw in the towel and accept the life of failure. Perhaps, even when you see a decline in your performance, you are apathetic because you have lost the appetite for living.

Conversely, you might not have mastered daily living and seem forever stuck in a life of little or no progress. Hence, you probably attribute the lack of progress in your life to fate or the circumstances of your birth. Accordingly, you do not try to do anything out of the ordinary to better yourself.

Your progress in life has stalled. So, you have wrongly concluded that you are unlikely to progress in your life no matter how much effort you put in. For these reasons, your grit is weakened, and your will for upward mobility is sapped. It is also likely that you think your life has peaked and have wrongly assumed you have reached your highest potential.

The difference between those who have failed in life and those who have succeeded is that, while the former easily give up, the latter do not, regardless of how dire their circumstances are. Neither do they become contented with what they have achieved and become complacent.

Instead, they persist in the face of failure. Furthermore, when, in their opinion, they have achieved something, they do not rest on their oars but continue to strive to reach higher goals.

Therefore, recognize that no matter which station you have attained in life or the direction your life is taking, there is always the hope that it can improve. No matter which direction your life is headed, you can arrest the situation and turn things around.

Benjamin Disraeli said, "Life is too short to be little." You see, you have what it takes to rediscover your mojo and turn your life around. You will discover what you have been missing as you read this book. Do not continue to "be little."

Awaken the giant in you by reading the book thoroughly and following the directions. Remember, this book can help you regain your confidence and refocus your life on becoming the *Superstar* you were meant to be. Go ahead; you are on your way to discovering what makes some people hotshots.

CHAPTER ONE
UNREALIZED POTENTIAL

I have seen slaves on horseback,
while princes go on foot like slaves.
Ecclesiastes 10:7

THE PRIZE FOR BAD JUDGMENTS

On a cold, snowy day, a man scuffled down a deserted road searching for shelter. He had been unsuccessful so far and looked beleaguered and brokenhearted. He was jobless, friendless, and homeless.

Not long before this time, he had a well-paying job, was happily married, and had friends and colleagues who cared about him. Now, he was down to the bare bones. The turnaround had happened when he cheated on his spouse and went away with another woman.

This adventure not only led to divorce and a broken home but also led to the loss of his job and personality. To add insult to injury, the woman for whom he left his wife also left when things started going downhill for him.

LIFE'S CONUNDRUMS

This man will suffer one bad break after another because of his initial fraught decision. His dilemma shows to what extent the business of life can be a puzzle. Not everybody will become homeless because of one bad decision.

However, we could each have problems because of some mistake. We each can spurn all the chances that come our way to leave us hanging on a thin thread with little or no hope.

On the other hand, you may not necessarily make a bad judgment but could still suffer in life. For example, some people, such as twins, were born on the same day with similar circumstances but could end up experiencing vastly different fortunes in life.

Conversely, many, like the homeless man, may end up on the wrong side of life because of wrong decisions. Others may not be able to take off because they carry hang-ups that continually push them to the bottom rungs of society.

The irony is that sometimes, their friends and acquaintances who were far inferior to them in all aspects of life, education, upbringing, and fortune, among others, may be doing better than they are. This can set anyone pondering why things have turned out how they have.

Some people may also suffer and underachieve because they cannot get along with anybody. They have burnt all their bridges and abused all the goodwill others had for them. For these reasons, they seem to be at odds with anything that can put their life back on track.

If you fall into any of these categories and have been wondering why your fortunes have turned sour, note the words of the teacher:

> "There is an evil I have seen under the sun. The sort of error that arises from a ruler. Fools are put in many high positions, while the rich occupy the low ones. I have seen slaves on horseback while princes go on foot like slaves." (Ecclesiastes 10:5-7).

This claim that the teacher makes is very true. Many people are groping in darkness because they have wasted the many opportunities that came their way in life or they have been unable to muster the courage to deal with the missiles that life throws at them.

Others are conflicted about who they are, their role in life, and what they can do to better their circumstances. Some people also assume that sitting down and not doing anything would still move them to the upper rungs of life's ladder.

Interestingly, any of the above reasons can condemn anybody to the bottom rungs of society when they could be further up on the ladder. Any person will be concerned if their progress in life seems to have stalled.

Understandably, these uncertainties that life throws at us are of great concern for the teacher who makes disturbing observations about humanity's fate.

He speaks about how clueless humans can be about what could happen to them in the future. He also infers that we are as helpless "as fish are caught in a cruel net, or birds are taken in a snare" (Ecclesiastes 9:12). The preacher's assertion proves that no individual is immune from life's difficulties and unexpected incidents.

ALL PEOPLE ARE PRONE TO MAKING MISTAKES

James, the elder, said that all humans stumble in many ways. He claimed that if anyone does not make a mistake in this life, he or she is perfect.[1] James was talking about speech, but it is an acceptable fact that it is not only what we say that can get us into trouble. We make mistakes in the vocations we choose the friends we choose, or even the spouses we choose. So, we should make allowances for our numerous shortcomings.

However, what we should not make room for is allowing our mistakes to put us down. If we take that line, it means we have given up on the fight and conceded defeat, even before the proper battle.

Accordingly, misfortunes and accidents will happen in life, but do not let those upset your goals. Some weak-willed people sometimes fold up under the weight of life's problems. They think that they are supposed to be somebody, and so discontent with their present state prevents them from making any strides to help themselves.

The writer, Laura B. Fortgang, recommends that people occupying positions they otherwise should not be occupying should use what she calls the 'why-what' approach in their quest for answers.

---

1. i. Cf. James 3:2-10

She contends that people should not be asking *why* they are not making it in life but should rather ask *what they can do* to change the situation they find themselves in. In other words, our approach to life should be one of finding solutions, not one of finding faults.

There are several obstacles to achievement in life. These include low self-esteem, indecision, a lack of resolve in life, or a willingness to easily give up when the going becomes tough. However, your courage will be proven if, in the face of adversity, you can still stand. If you do not crumble and fold up in the face of hardship, you can surely make it through the next step.

POSSIBILITIES FOR RECOVERY

For all those who have hit a snag, it is not only time to ride out the storm but to begin to take the necessary steps to stop the inertia. Your possibilities for recovery start with you. The creator has laid down the rules for any of his children to be successful in this life. However, he will not force his will on any of us. It is up to any person who finds his or her way foggy to ask for his providence to abandon the life of failure, disappointment, and even disaster and return to the path of progress and improvement.

You need to take concrete steps instead of being rendered docile and inactive as if crushed by the weight of the many problems you have encountered. Take courage and know that there is still hope for your redemption.

GOD'S MASTER PLAN FOR YOU

First, if you have been underachieving, know that it is not the will of the creator for you. His will is for you to thrive. In your state of hopelessness, don't you sometimes feel the consciousness of God's presence urging and prodding you not to give up?

Surely, the creator would want you to keep fighting because survival is within your reach. He has a master plan for your life. It is only when you realize it that you can get back to winning ways. This master plan is available to everybody. However, it is those who are in constant communication with him who gain an understanding of this plan and its workings. This plan will not only lead you to see your deficiencies but will prompt you to rely on God's providence.

Second, know that it is never too late to begin a new venture or to take a new course to turn your life around. There is nothing like too young or too old. No matter what stage one has reached in life, there is always something good present. Let us hold fast to that which is good and will bring us life.

Gloria Copeland sees a purpose in the master plan that God has put in place for everyone. She claims that not only is this plan purposeful but is also unique to every single individual.[2] This means that nothing that has happened or will happen is of chance.

What this suggests is that, everyone on earth is born with his or her own purposely designed blueprint. There will never be another you. After your death, the creator is not going to duplicate your blueprint in another individual.

Wayne Dyer perceives that "our earliest personality traits and predilections are expressed because they represent our highest selves."[3] He assumes that when we are young, we cleave to God and remain connected. According to him, as we mature, we seize the "chance to edge God out and assume the mantle of the false self, which is the ego."[4]

INDIVIDUALS UNIQUELY ENDOWED

If Dyer is to be properly interpreted, we will surmise that we are created with unique qualities that only get tainted as we go through life. Life has a way of throwing us hard punches and derailing our forward march. However, we can still stand if we are willing to continue fighting and not throw in the towel.

Since each of us is unique, we must nurture this trait, which only we can remodel. If you can do a good job in this period of nurture, you will blossom into a beautiful and true replica of the person God created you to be.

---

2. iii. Copeland, Gloria. *God's Master Plan for Your Life: Ten Keys to Fulfilling Your Destiny.* New York: G. P. Putman's Sons, 2008, 1.

3. Dyer, Wayne W. *I Can See Clearly Now.* Carlsbad, California: Hay House Inc., 2014, 6

4. Ibid.

In the *Graveyard Book*, the English writer Neil Gaiman argued that every person has infinite potential. That means individuals can bring into being anything they can dream about.[5] That potential is not limited to a few gifted individuals. Rather, any person who has breath possesses it.

Sir Isaac Newton was the one who found out that objects at rest have potential energy while those in motion have kinetic energy. What Newton found out in his experiments and what Gaiman wrote about confirms that people have something within them that could be untapped. Supposedly, that dormant energy, if ignited, can change your world.

Truly, your talents are waiting to be unearthed to make you the superstar you were meant to be. But until now, you may have bought into some false information given to you by some negative force that you will not amount to anything.

Such negative and self-belittling words mainly come from people intent on hurting us but sometimes also unwarily from loved ones such as our parents. Since negative criticisms are unavoidable, you should find a viable way to stem any sloppiness in your performance.

FACTORS THAT AFFECT INDIVIDUAL DEVELOPMENT

Though the Bible asserts that we are created perfect, in the image of God, there are mitigating forces. There are the hereditary factors, which, to a larger extent, are responsible for who we are and those we encounter growing up. While our surroundings do not necessarily guarantee success, they have more than a fair share of influence on who we are. If you grow up in a rich environment, your chances of making it up the social ladder are greater than someone who grows up with little or no resources.

Likewise, there are some things that we pick up in our nurture. These include slothfulness and envy, identity crisis, fear of intimacy, inability to control one's temper, sexual struggles, or a craving for anything new. Never

---

5. v. http://www.goodreads.com/quotes/tag/potential accessed April 11, 2015

delude yourself into thinking you were born with such traits as these if you have them. When a child is born, he or she carries none of these deficiencies. However, as the child grows, they pick up such behavior patterns from peers and other acquaintances.

Besides these two factors, hereditary and environmental, peer influence can also be a big factor. If one is unlucky to team up with the wrong crowd, what they will learn will be drunkenness, drugs, and, in the worst-case scenario, may end up in prostitution. On the other hand, with friends who love and fear God, this same person will end up strong, vibrant, God-fearing, and a big influence on the society in which he or she lives.

However, for many others, their inability to achieve their objectives in life stem from other reasons. First, they are so critical of others and negative about everything. In their cynicism, they are not only excessively burdensome but are also overly awkward in their relationships. Furthermore, they are rude and blunt in their dealings.

Second, they have a damaging appraisal of self, a distrustful estimation of others, and an undesirable assessment of the world. They never see anything positive and affirmative about themselves and the world around them. This negativity tends to hinder any personal growth and achievement. Not only does such an attitude affect others in society, but it also hinders their personal development.

Third, they are so passive in society and have very little worry about anything except those that pertain directly to them. For all they care, even if a wall is falling in it is not their worry. Their interest is so narrow that nothing tends to concern them.

Interestingly, whatever shortcomings you are bedeviled with, you can still change for the better. For example, the apostle Paul is portrayed as a firebrand in his approach to preaching the gospel. However, in certain situations, he was accommodating to achieve his goal.

Margaret Mitchell, a theologian, claims that Paul developed 'the language of condescension.'[6] She argues that this approach that Paul took with

---

6. cf. Mitchell, Margaret M. Paul and the Rhetoric of Reconciliation: An Exegetical Investigation of the Language and Composition of 1 Corinthians. Tübingen: J.C.B. Mohr (P. Siebeck), 1991. In 1Cor. 9:19-23, Paul displays rhetoric of condescension, by appearing weak for the weak and strong for the strong in order to remain relevant to the people whom he sought to reach.

his non-Jewish audience made him a success among them. Mitchell's claim does not mean we ought to be patronizing in our dealings with others to gain acceptance. Rather, it suggests we must design suitable ways to deal with others.

Additionally, prevailing trends in the world today underscore our interdependence. Less than two hundred years ago, something that happened in one corner of the world remained a problem in that area. However, now, when something happens in India, there will be Americans, Australians, Nigerians, or Germans who will be affected. For example, the 2016 Ebola outbreak in some West African countries and the 2020 Coronavirus that originated in China became a worldwide problem.

The world is a global village, so a reclusive lifestyle is no longer tenable. The implication is that anyone interested in only self should get out there and become an active member of the society in which they live.

It is of interest to our world that every human plays his or her part in ensuring peace, tranquility, and progress. If such a thing can happen, it will require that we each ignite our God-given talent to make positive contributions to our world.

So that you may no longer be groping around, let the word of God be a lamp to your feet and a light to your path. The second stanza of Charles Wesley's hymn, "Captain of Israel's Host and Guide," assures the believer that if God's unerring spirit leads one, that person will not stray in the desert, nor will he or she need full direction because they will not fail to find God's "providential way." Truly, if the divine light directs your paths, you will surely not miss your way. You will always find your way home because your creator is watching for you.

If you can grasp the essence of such an action, it will turn your life on its ears and propel you into a new horizon you hardly dreamt about. It will turn your life of mediocrity into one of a Superstar. Countless numbers of people have discovered the truth about their God-given abilities and have thus been able to turn their lives around. Today, it is your turn to acknowledge your innate strengths, which the creator has imbued you with so that you can become a Superstar.

CHAPTER TWO

WORK HARD, WORK SMART, STAY FOCUSED AND SUCCEED

"I'm a greater believer in luck, and I find the harder I work the more I have of it"
Thomas Jefferson

THE CONSEQUENCES OF ONE'S WORK ETHIC

Jamal, an unemployed African American man, lived in the Birmingham, Alabama, suburb of Irondale. He had been in and out of work and ran out of unemployment benefits. Thus, he incurred a large debt by falling on payday loans with high interest. His financial situation had led him into a state of despair, causing him to blame the people and the system, which he assumed were responsible for his woes.

The problem with Jamal was not caused by anything outside himself as he made it look. His problems were laziness, ill temper, and greed. This behavior put him at odds with everyone. Besides, he dropped out of High School and was unsuccessful at the GED examinations.

Furthermore, whichever job he got, he could not learn the skills needed for that job quickly enough. For these same reasons, he could not hold a job for more than six months. The longest he had ever spent at a job was five months. Accordingly, he was always in dire need of money to pay his bills. With this plethora of problems, it is no wonder he found himself in his present mess.

People like Jamal will always find themselves in a quagmire regarding finances, and why not? They are not willing to stay committed to a job, nor are they smart about what they can do to achieve something in life. As a result, they will always be saddled with bills they cannot pay.

THE HUMAN QUEST FOR SUCCESS

One truth about humans is that we want to succeed in life. We want to have the best house, drive the flashiest car, and buy whatever we desire at any time. However, like Jamal, you cannot achieve the success you want if you do not have a strong work ethic because success is undoubtedly the result of fruitful work. If you should ask anybody who has achieved anything in this life how they got to where they are, they will answer that they have been committed to their work.

Success covers a movement from one station in life to another and usually involves work, determination, and belief. If you can make it in life, you will not only need to believe in your talents and worth but also have staying power and the ability to work hard.

The right amount of these three ingredients would present the perfect recipe for success. The wise king once said, "The soul of the sluggard craves and gets nothing, while the soul of the diligent is richly supplied" (Proverbs 13:4).

Thus, the hallmark of Superstars is a focused and determined work ethic, the willingness to take leaps of faith, and the ability to hold on when the signs are not good and everybody is telling them to quit. All achievers have certain characteristics. They do not crumble in the face of adversity. They view problems as stepping stones instead of as stumbling blocks.

They work hard to transform challenges into stimuli, the bad and ugly, into something good and attractive. They work to leave examples for others to see obstacles as challenges that could be overcome.

If you are successful, you need to separate work from leisure. You must know when to work and when to take a vacation. The implication is that you must be committed to what you do. Moreover, your willingness to take up responsibility is key to success. If you are a person who fails to take responsibility or lacks trustworthiness, you will achieve minimal success both in your chosen profession and in life generally.

EQUIP YOURSELF WITH THE APPROPRIATE SKILL

Another key principle you may need to master in any job is to learn the skills associated with that trade. For example, the preacher, the teacher, the actor, or the politician who wants to excel in his or her chosen profession needs to master the essential elements of his or her respective field.

Although some people are born with prodigious abilities, we cannot discount the fact that skill acquisition depends on ability and nurture. Therefore, any individual's talents could be nurtured through a deliberate and consistent educational process that normally begins from the cradle to the grave.

The Roman philosopher Quintilian showed that it was the practice of ancient Romans to acquire rhetorical skills through early training.[7] His assertion underscores the immense usefulness of how the proper skills can make you a master in your chosen field. It also highlights the need for constant and sustained practice on your part if you can attain your goals in life.

If you can work hard to be flawless in your speech, faultless in your performance, and perfect in your relations, doors will open for you. If you are a preacher, you should work not only on your speaking skills but also on your public relations. Let me be frank: in today's world, people are less receptive to the gospel message. If you have this knowledge, take a leaf from the ancient people of Rome and Greece who strived to be the best in their chosen fields.

A church historian, O. C. Edwards, credited these two groups for their mastery of oratory, from which the modern public speaking platform sprang.

---

7. Quintilian 1-2:67.

Therefore, learn from these ancient people and improve your skills to perform on an even bigger platform. Make it your goal to communicate the gospel effectively to your congregation and the larger audience who remain skeptical of the message of Christ.

Additionally, mastery of human relations will give you a better chance of sharing the gospel message with your congregation and the larger audience. In this way, others will see you as a genuine ambassador of Christ.

If you are a politician, you need to master two things: public speaking and human relations. The world knows how easily Barack Obama was swept into power because of his speech-making skills. While we cannot say whether that was something he was born with, one thing we can be sure of is that he constantly practiced fine-tuning his talent.

Besides your speaking skills, as a politician, always get close to your constituents so that you can address their needs. This will authenticate your speeches and the many functions you will perform on their behalf.

The next group, actors and actresses, also need to practice continuously to gain mastery of their subject. The skill you will need for acting that pertains to this discussion is mastering whatever scripts you are given.

However, gaining a mastery of the script is but the beginning. You also need to be innovative in acting out what the script says. For this to be possible, your imagination will come into play. In the same way, craftsmanship requires repeated practice in that trade to gain more silkiness.

When it comes to building relationships, you should practice a way of addressing people. Your language should be simple and on target to effectively communicate with others. In that way, it will aid your listeners to perceive and make sense of what you are saying. Consider three things in your interactions: imaginative, sensitive, and considerate.

Similarly, if you are a teacher, you should know beforehand what you intend to teach so that your classroom presentations are interesting and well-informed for your students.

A good teacher goes into the classroom with appropriate notes, proper teaching aids, and the readiness to teach. There is this well-known adage that 'practice makes perfect.' Therefore, your private study before going out to teach is very important.

You must study hard to pass your tests if you are a student. This is even truer for sportsmen and women than for most trades. The difference between an excelling athlete and an average athlete is the number of hours they each put into their practice.

THE SHINING EXAMPLE OF JACKIE ROBINSON

Many gifted sportsmen have fluffed their lines probably because they spent less time in practice and more time chasing fun. Conversely, some sportsmen and women take their training regimen seriously and become unbeatable in their chosen fields.

The person who demonstrated this phenomenon was Jackie Robinson (1919-1972), the first African American to play a significantly prominent role in major league baseball.

In 1947, when Jackie Robinson signed for the Brooklyn Dodgers, he became the first black American in the major leagues. In that same year, he was named the Rookie of the Year.

Before joining the Dodgers, he played for the Montreal Royals, leading the International League with a 0.349 average and 40 stolen bases.

National League MVP followed Robinson's initial achievements in 1949 and a World Series champ in 1955. In a period when blacks did not have the same rights as whites or even people of other races, Robinson worked his socks off amidst the taunts and boos that accompanied all his performances.

He is believed to have said, "A life is not important except in the impact it has on other lives." With this as his mantra, he worked hard on the field to perfect his play and off the field to advocate for equal rights for his fellow blacks in all spheres of life.

His resistance to discrimination earned him arrests and court martials, but he was unrelenting in what he stood for. Robinson's success was attributed to hard work and the resolve not to yield to pressure. It is said that long after his playing mates were gone from practice sessions, he would continue to do more practice. Robinson's example shows that with hard work, you, too, can be a great hit in your chosen profession.

This need for hard work was underscored by Quintilian in his audacious claim that "those who make an effort to get to the top will climb higher than those who from the start despair of emerging where they want to be and stop right at the foot of the hill."[8]

Though this claim pertains to speech, it applies to any field of human endeavor. Whatever profession you have chosen, if you put in extra time to develop the skills needed, you will surely rise to the peak of that chosen profession and become a Superstar.

Let me sound a word of caution here. Please know that if you can attain proficient skills for your chosen trade, it will not happen overnight, so do not give in to desperation if things are not happening as you imagined. Do not give up on your desire to improve by developing the requisite skills you need for your trade.

Furthermore, give it your very best whenever you are presented with an opportunity. In that way, people will take you seriously and present more opportunities to you in the future.

EVERY PROFESSION EQUALLY IMPORTANT

You will think that the glamour associated with success will motivate people to be committed to what they do. At least we saw Jamal, who was unmotivated to work, notwithstanding all his financial woes. However, not all underachievers are lazy or intemperate. Some people find themselves in this group simply because they perceive their job as inconsequential.

A story is told of Sir Michael Costa, a great orchestra conductor of the 19th Century. One day, he was conducting a rehearsal for a concert joined by a great choir. This was a big event with all the instruments needed for a good orchestra present. There were woodwind, percussion, brass, and string

---

8. Quintilian 1-2:61.

instruments. In many orchestras, the woodwind instruments comprise three flutes, a piccolo, three oboes, an English horn, and three clarinets.

On the night in question, all the woodwind instruments, as well as the other groups of instruments, were present. To the untrained ear, the presentation was going great, but suddenly, Sir Costa stopped the performance and shouted to the piccolo player, "Why have you stopped playing?"

The piccolo player timidly stepped out and said that he felt his instrument was unimportant and that its sound was drowned out by the other bigger instruments. To this, Sir Costa replied, "Oh no, play on because without the piccolo, there is no orchestra."

After this admonition, the piccolo player played his best, and the performance thereafter was overwhelming.[9] The piccolo is half the size of a standard flute but plays the highest note among all the woodwind instruments. Without it, no instrument sets the tune for the orchestra.

Many people are like that Piccolo player. Wrongly, they presume that their contribution to total world output is underwhelming. Such people fail to realize that the collective effort of everybody culminates in the big world output. Hence, they stop doing anything positive to contribute to overall human productivity.

People who harbor such thoughts are lazy in their approach to work. However, just as the piccolo player thought his instrument was insignificant, you should recognize that every occupation, no matter its contribution to overall human productivity, is vital for the survival of society.

Let us take the work of a housekeeper, for example. If there is going to be a party, everybody might see her work as the least significant and may ignore her if there is an award to be given. However, if the housekeeper refuses to do his or her work, nobody can come to the party and enjoy it because of the filth that will be around.

This underscores the fact that no one occupation is more important than another. This fact was brought home by Jesus in one of his parables. This parable, the parable of the bags of gold, brings to the fore the benefit of showing commitment at work and using any talent, no matter how little.[10]

---

9. The Story of the Piccolo Player<www.storiesforpreaching.com accessed August 12, 2015
10. Read Matthew 25:14-28 for the full story.

In this parable, a man going on a journey allocated his property to his servants as capital. He gave out this wealth according to the abilities he had seen in those servants. To one, he gave five bags of gold, to another two bags, and to the last, one bag. After distributing his wealth in that manner, he went on his journey.

The man who had received five bags of gold went at once, put his money to work, and gained five bags more. So also, the one with two bags of gold gained two more. But the man who had received one bag went off, dug a hole in the ground, and hid his master's money.

There are several lessons to be learned from this parable. The major lesson is that those servants who put their talents to work achieved a proportionate return, while those who did not use their talent got nothing.

Not only does the parable underscore the importance of hard work, but it also shows that every person has an inborn ability that can always be ignited. Those who can make it in life and gain recognition as Superstars are the ones who discover their potential strengths and weaknesses and can use those strengths while at the same time working to turn their weaknesses into strengths.

As the parable portrayed, not all people possess the same abilities. However, in our own way, there is something we can do if we only put what we have to use. Those people who fail in this life are those who fail to put their talents to work. You may have talents that are unique to you and may remain untapped. The way to release this gift is through training.

TRAINING CAN MAKE A DIFFERENCE

Regarding skills attainment in one's chosen profession, it is a well-known fact that there are naturally gifted people. Those will always have a head start because they do not need as much tutoring as people with little ability.

Nevertheless, if you find what you love to do but are deficient in the required skills, adopt a study pattern to help you acquire proficiency. You owe it to yourself and society to undertake such a study to improve yourself and society.

There are two forms of study that you can adopt to improve your skills. You do not necessarily need formal education to excel in any undertaking. However, in some professions, a college education is needed. If this is your lot, you can make the pursuit of formal education a priority. These days, there are many online courses available in almost any profession. Therefore, if you need a job to finance your studies, you can continue to work and acquire a meaningful education.

The second form of study is the on-the-job acquisition of skills. Always ensure you are abreast of trends in your profession by reading articles about the latest developments associated with it. You can also learn skills you do not yet have from fellow workers or can always get more on-the-job training.

Moreover, put in a daily regimen to ensure your present performance is always better than any preceding. Draw up a daily schedule, which will serve as a checklist to always monitor your progress. That way, you will remain on course to achieving your goals.

DON'T DISCOUNT PROVIDENCE IN YOUR PERSONAL DEVELOPMENT

To vouch for the influence of education on your well-being as a person does not necessarily dismiss the effects of providence on personal development. In the novel Jane Eyre, Charlotte Brontë wrote, "It is a pity that doing one's best does not always answer." Brontë's observation is true because human ability has limitations.

Rather, doing your best and praying that God would help your labor bear fruit could lead to achievement. Working hard demands a toughness that can withstand all the difficulties that will come your way. You will surely fail in any endeavor if you bend with the least resistance. Know that God's help is available to people who do not give up despite intense adversity.

The Bible is emphatic in its claim that without the blessings of God, all the work that one does is in vain. That means that if we could consolidate our gains in any work we do, we should trust our work to God because he is the one who grants success.

Embarking on personal self-improvement through study and a determined desire to succeed holds several imaginative threads together. These threads hold our link to family and friends together and help us find our place in society. Furthermore, they give meaning to life and help us develop our own unique identities. Moreover, it gives us the confidence to deal with others we encounter daily.

NEVER GIVE UP WITHOUT A FIGHT

In his book *Outrageous, Contagious Joy*, author and pastor Ed Young explores how one can achieve a fulfilling life. He assumes that some people give up easily without a fight. They do not probe hard enough when things do not turn out how they want. They fail to turn their "what if?" into "what's next?"

He argues that life is not about giving up when apparent failure stares someone in the face. He wrote: "Discovering the great life God wants for you is all about dreaming about what is possible by examining the big picture." In his opinion, "so often we get stuck in the mud and the mundane issues of life rather than seeing what is truly possible. We feel like there's something more out there, but don't know how to get it. We know there's more to life but don't know where to turn."[11]

Isn't that the feeling you sometimes have? That you have not maximized your strengths? That there is more to life than you are making of it? Don't you sometimes beat yourself on something you were supposed to do but failed to do? I am sure that you do not derive any satisfaction from your inaction.

If you feel that way, know you are not alone. We all feel that way sometimes. Therefore, instead of despairing, put in concrete work to arrest the situation. Hold on to this quest for self-improvement, and it will give you the push to believe in your ability to right the wrongs to ensure greater future accomplishments.

When you get to that stage, you and others should see visible improvements in your life. These should boost your confidence levels and set clear

---

11. Young, Ed. *Outrageous, Contagious Joy: Five Big Questions to Help You Discover One Great Life*. New York: The Berkley Publishing Group, 2007, 1-2.

markers in the sand to differentiate you from others. The markers perform two things on your behalf: they help other people form positive opinions about you, and they begin to trust you with more responsibility. These markers are what people who study group dynamics term "idiosyncrasy credits."

BUILDING YOUR IDIOSYNCRASY CREDITS

Idiosyncrasy credit is how others see us and usually mirrors how we see ourselves. If our self-perception is positive, others will similarly see us that way. A positive perception implies higher credits, whilst a negative perception suggests lower credits.

The way to secure higher credits should begin with your projection of a positive self-image as well as the development of certain time-tested principles. These principles, which are outlined below, will positively impact your idiosyncrasy credits.

The steps you can take to build your idiosyncrasy credit should begin with developing your confidence in tackling tasks. When you have confidence in your ability, it will aid you in performing any tasks associated with your trade.

Your confidence building should align with acquiring a good work ethic and an unwavering desire not to compromise on those ethics. Next, acquire and polish the skills needed for your trade. You should not slack in this task until you are, without a doubt, a master in the technique and language of your profession.

As Solomon wrote in his Proverbs: "Do you see a man skillful in his work? He will stand before kings; he will not stand before obscure men" (Proverbs 22:29). Moreover, as Thomas Edison once alluded, there are no born geniuses, but people who put in ninety percent work with ten percent inspiration to become irresistible.

Another measure that will put you on an upward trajectory is to resolve to never quit in the middle of a project. Quitting will damage your idiosyncrasy credit instead of building it up. You will be viewed as a failure, not a success. However, if you remain tenacious and refuse to give in to setbacks, you will prevail.

Furthermore, you should seek out mentorship relationships with people who have already excelled in your profession so that you can fashion your work after them. Also, don't compete with people at or below your level. Rather, always strive to be at par with or even better than those who are the leaders in your profession.

If you take these steps to increase your idiosyncrasy credits, nobody can ignore you. Not only will you become irreplaceable, but it will propel you to greater heights and make you unstoppable.

CHAPTER THREE

AVOID PROCRASTINATION— IT HAS STALLING EFFECTS

"Do what you have to do today because you don't owe tomorrow; therefore, to say I will do it tomorrow is to infringe on God's territory; wait till he gives you tomorrow, then you can do whatever you have to do. Until then, maximize your today, for you may not have tomorrow."
Ebenezer Alabi · Head Pastor—Mission of Hope Ministries

PROCRASTINATION, THE STONEWALL EFFECT

Jane, a suburban Chicago mother, was thrown into a state of surprise but also regret to see her classmate anchor a major television program. Her regret came from the fact she and her friend had both planned to go into broadcasting after college.

Whilst her friend went ahead to apply, she kept postponing her action and never put in an application. Thus, due to her knack for procrastinating, Jane, a valedictorian who graduated at the top of her high school class, now works at a fast-food restaurant while her lesser-endowed friend is a major television presenter.

Since her youth, Jane had always been putting off anything she had to do. Now, older and on her own, she still procrastinates. Her lack of promptness always saddled her with unpaid bills, which gathered late fees, further reducing her spending power.

This problem of procrastination, which Jane and countless others have, interrupts personal development and stifles future progress. To stem such a trend, prompt action is always needed to arrest the slightest hint of delayed action before its negative effects become impactful.

PROCRASTINATION: THE CAUSES, THE SUSTAINING DYNAMICS

There are many and varied reasons why people procrastinate. The first could be attributed to improper goal setting. In this case, the goals are too broad and improperly defined. In such instances, one tends to waddle about as somebody wading through mud, not knowing where he is headed.

Another person may not set goals at all, so they have nothing they are working towards. Incidentally, if you have no goals, you do not have any markers to alert you. That state can also contribute to procrastination.

For some people, their problem is in how they manage their time. Since they lack time management skills, they do not know what they should do at one time or another. Have you heard the saying 'time and tide waits for no one?' If you do not manage your time well, you can never go back to reclaim it.

Paul warned the believers in Ephesus: "Be very careful, then, how you live—not as unwise but as wise, making the most of every opportunity, because the days are evil. Therefore do not be foolish, but understand what the Lord's will is" (Ephesians 5:15-17).

Yet, for others, their bane is multi-tasking. They take on too many tasks that, in the end, nothing is accomplished. When you combine multiple tasks in hopes of getting a lot done, you may end up doing nothing because your attention will be distracted.

For some other people, the reason they procrastinate is their inability to say no. Such people, even in the middle of a project, will stop to do something else for somebody. Since they have this ineptitude, they are always saddled with uncompleted projects.

THE RESULT OF PROCRASTINATION

If it remains unchecked, procrastination can become a controlling factor in your life. Thus, it is very important that at the first sign of any desire to procrastinate, you put the brakes on it before it blossoms into something uncontrollable.

Otherwise, it could become a major obstacle in your life. The fact is that none of the things that control you can have such devastating effects as those that are wrought by procrastination. Procrastination can be responsible for a person not landing the right job, losing out on opportunities in life, or even, in matters of faith, failing to surrender their lives to God.

The writer of Hebrews took a leaf from the history of the people of Israel, the generation that passed through the wilderness and never made it to the Promised Land. He uses that analogy to urge his readers to take prompt action on how they relate to God and other vital life decisions.

It may be lost on you that everything has a window of opportunity. If you fail to take that chance, it may never present itself again. Therefore, as you go through life, you must watch out for those moments so that when they happen, you will take hold and not let them pass you by.

The window of opportunity opens at various stages in life. When you are young and energetic, there is a window that will open, which only the fledgling and active can peep through. Therefore, when you allow those opportunities to pass you by when they open again in your old age, you might not be suitable to seize them since they are age-sensitive.

THE ADVANTAGES OF DECISIVENESS

There are several advantages in decisiveness. If you are decisive and prompt, you can get things done. It helps you focus on the big picture to achieve your end goal. Again, decisive people are never delusional in thinking things can be achieved overnight. Instead, they realize that they have work to do to achieve goals and milestones. Thus, they labor incessantly to reach their goal.

Since decisive people can get things done, they earn the respect of their peers. Before long, others entrust them with more responsibility. It is commonplace that when your peers see you as an achiever, you will easily win their vote to become their leader. Solomon said, "The hand of the diligent will rule, while the slothful will be put to forced labor" (Proverbs 12:24).

Decisive people often have an abundant supply. As Solomon wrote: "Love not sleep, lest you come to poverty; open your eyes, and you will have plenty of bread" (Proverbs 20:13). Therefore, because the decisive does not loiter around, they are always richly supplied.

It is worthy to note that a person who has the propensity to keep on postponing never gets anything done. However, if this same person becomes proactive, he or she can accomplish much. This same reason is responsible for people who are decisive in accomplishing great things in their lives.

Thus, resoluteness is the key to achievement because the decisive person does not postpone what needs to be done now until a future date. They are aware that any affinity they show to procrastination may hinder them from carrying out tasks for which they do not doubt completing successfully. Furthermore, they are aware that any knack to procrastinate will rob them of the opportunity they are sure to carry out without any qualms.

Again, the decisive person agrees with the popular saying that 'Rome was not built in a day'. Therefore, they consider that since no big venture can be accomplished in a day, they are not detracted when a project's completion becomes protracted. Instead, they keep momentum by doing a little each day to build on their success incrementally.

WAYS TO STOP PROCRASTINATION

Procrastination is a learned behavior that we pick up in our nurture. We learn everything in our lives through repeated action. Just as you can learn to procrastinate through repeated action, you can similarly train yourself to be prompt in your ways. Thus, there are viable steps you can take to stop postponing what needs to be done. The first step is to have written down goals and the determination to stick to them.

Clearly stated goals will give you direction, and the resolve to see them through will help you complete tasks. Remember, these goals should not be too broad or too vague to make them unrealistic to achieve. Second, these goals will help you have a clear vision of where you are headed, as well as what you want to achieve.

Next, avoid any desire to daydream about what you want out of life. Daydreaming translates you into a world of fantasy. Therefore, be alert to your vision in life, which you have set in those written goals, and never veer from your forward march.

Another thing is that you should never look at your circumstances and put limitations on your ability to undertake a task. Always believe that it is well within your means to tackle and complete a task. Likewise, do not make excuses for yourself as to why a certain job has not been completed. Do not postpone what needs to be done today to tomorrow.

Moreover, look for, and arrest any poor time management skills. A good way to build healthy time management is to set short-term goals that can be completed at set times. Finally, learn to put your priorities right, to make the problem of procrastination ancient history. Setting priorities right could include saying no to external requests when you feel your schedule is tight.

THE RIGHT TIME TO ACT

It is irrefutable that any person who habitually postpones what needs to be done will be trapped in perpetual failure. Hence, if you have such shortcomings, you must admit that your non-committal attitude will negatively affect any progress you can make. Thus, when you discover this shortfall in your life, you must determine that once you commit to doing something, you will not change course. If you can keep to such commitments, you will gradually break any stranglehold that procrastination has on your life.

Life is full of difficulties. Those who can withstand those worries are the ones who make it. Others easily fold up and crumble in the face of glitches.

Alexander Dumas said: "When you compare the sorrows of real life to the pleasures of the imaginary one, you will never want to live again, only to dream forever."[12]

Dumas is right, don't we all sometimes muse about our misfortunes and refuse to engage? Sometimes instead of identifying problems and tackling them headlong, don't we turn to imagine what could have been, instead of devising schemes and plans that could redeem our situation?

Instead of contemplating what could have been, it is time to be proactive. Recognize that any inclination to hurry through assignments will always give you an unsatisfactory product. Therefore, give yourself adequate time to prepare for any task you undertake.

Do not hastily give up on a venture if you fail because, in most success stories, the protagonists succeed only after failing time and again. Winston Churchill said, "Success consists of going from failure to failure without loss of enthusiasm."[13]

Therefore, if you are a person who easily throws in the towel when failure stares you in the face, your lot will simply be to procrastinate. You do so because you think you might do better at a future date. Sometimes you may need to suspend something that needs doing to give attention to certain urgent matters. However, such actions should not be protracted to avoid delaying any earlier assignments.

Remember, life is like a moving train. People get on the train at different stations to go to the same or different destinations. Assuming you must get to a place but keep on postponing which train to get on, by the time you firmly decide, all the scheduled trains might have passed. The option that may be left to you is to walk.

Similarly, in life. If you fail to take opportunities when they come, you may be unable to make meaningful headway when you finally make up your mind to act. The difference between life and this analogy, however, is that no matter how late you are to realize shortfalls in your life, you can always act. Whilst you might not be able to achieve as much as you could have done if you had started earlier, it is still worth the try.

---

12. http://www.goodreads.com/author/quotes/4785.Alexandre_Dumas accessed April 11, 2015

13. http://www.brainyquote.com/quotes/authors/w/winston_churchill.html accessed September 3, 2015

CHAPTER FOUR

FEAR HAS CRIPPLING EFFECTS

*"Too many of us are not living our dreams
because we are living our fears"*
Les Brown

FEAR, AN INTEGRAL PART OF HUMAN PERSONALITY

Jenny, the once buoyant and fearless teenager from Buda Texas, near Austin was now a nervous wreck. Her condition had been induced by the sudden death of her mother in a motor accident. That tragedy certainly made Jenny fearful of everything around her. When she went to bed, she would leave the light on, thinking, in the dark, something terrible would happen to her.

Notwithstanding that fear is an integral part of the human personality and makeup, for people like Jenny, it can be carried to extremes. Even those of us who are not normally afraid can still have some amount of fear. We can be afraid of anything that does not look like us or behave like us, such as corpses and ghosts.

There are many things that cause us to be afraid. These include a reaction to a past traumatic state, uncertainty about the future, or an imminent threat from disease or war. The apprehensions explain our fear of heights, water, or blood, among others.

POSITIVE AND NEGATIVE FEAR

In some strange way, some amount of fear is vital for human survival. Fear, therefore, may not necessarily be bad because sometimes it is for the good of a person. In its goodness, it warns people off or gets them out of danger. Conversely, in its vileness, it has regressive effects. Fear, therefore, can be classified as negative or positive depending on the context in which it is applied.

The book of Proverbs says that the fear of God is the beginning of wisdom. That type of fear is positive fear. Fear that is positive is akin to how the human nervous system works. It helps us, as humans, to live a life that is possibly free from trouble. Any person in his or her right mind does not handle red fire because his or her senses tell him or her not to hold it or even go close so that he or she would not get burned by the fire.

Therefore, fear can be inherently good. The worth of positive fear is to keep humans from evil acts. It reinforces in us the desire to look out for one another. On the other hand, negative fear is the type that is fundamentally useless to its subject. What negative fear does is cripple the unwary and make him ineffective in any of life's endeavors.

Negative fears, which are mostly classified as phobias, such as the fear of heights, darkness, or blood, prevent individuals from carrying out vital functions either for their course or for the good of society.

The effect of positive fear is to strengthen our relationship with God, family, friends, and the larger society. These strengthened relationships enable us to smoothly navigate the challenges of life. When you have strengthened relationships, it becomes easy for you to relate with others, and you are always guaranteed their assistance.

Contrarily, the effect of negative fear is to erode any confidence you have in yourself and others. It is the reason for the many conflicts we see in the family and society. It erodes the trust that can exist between groups or individuals. The control which negative fear exerts on its subjects is like that which a bully exerts on a weakling. On the other hand, the freedom that positive fear makes available to the individual is the ability to take hold of her circumstances and do great things for herself.

Due to its draining effect, negative fear requires drastic action on the part of individuals and groups to fight off its influence. Whether working for ourselves or in groups, we need to ward off any tendencies predisposing us to negative fear. That was what Franklin D Roosevelt did on behalf of the American people when the whole nation was threatened by a fear that could have wiped out any confidence the people had to make something out of their lives.

Roosevelt was president from 1933 to 1945 at the height of the Great Depression, at a time when the world was in turmoil, the time World War II was going on. The situation in the USA and in the rest of the world was bleak, even hopeless. Hopelessness was everywhere. He was the leader America needed at that time in its history. He saw the monstrosity of the problems confronting the people, and he led them not to run but to tackle them headlong.

At his inauguration, he spoke about the depression and the prospect of turning the U.S. economy around. He told the people: "The only thing we have to fear, is fear itself!" Americans took his message and worked hard to achieve a prosperous economy, which we enjoy today. Through his words and actions, Roosevelt underscored the power of human words.

THE CRIPPLING EFFECTS OF FEAR

The lesson from Roosevelt's address to the people of his time gives credence to the fact that fear need not become the major stumbling block that it sometimes is. There are many individuals and groups who have not been as fortunate to hear words that would help them deal with their fears.

If you are a victim of negative fear, look for avenues where you can address that shortfall in your life before it spreads into something out of control. Out-of-control fear usually has a spiraling effect. It will not only make an abled-body and healthy individual fearful and timid but also inept.

The following story illustrates the crippling effects fear can have if it is allowed to fester. A man was imprisoned on a lonely island for thirty-seven years. For all his years of incarceration, the only person he saw was a mean-looking jailer who would bring him food once a day.

One day, after thirty-seven years, he decided to kill the jailer when he opened the door to come in so that he could make his way out to freedom. As he rehearsed his plan to murder the jailer, he discovered the obvious. His door had been unlocked all the time he was there.

On further exploration, there was another startling discovery: there was a getaway boat sitting on the lake with a full fuel tank, food, and clothing; everything he needed to get away from his prison and to safety.

The irony is that for all the thirty-seven years that he was imprisoned, not only was his door not under lock, but also the getaway boat was ready for his use. What kept him in there was the fear of the mean-looking warden. You see, many of us have been imprisoned by our thoughts. We cannot break loose even though we have embers of greatness within us. Therefore, going by what Roosevelt said, fear is the only enemy preventing our breakout season.

Another story comes from the history of Israel. After their rescue from slavery in Egypt, they wandered the desert. During that period, they benefitted from God's providence and goodwill. Nevertheless, when it came time to take possession of the land God had promised them, they raised objections. They would not proceed because they were afraid of giants who lived on that land.

Similarly, many people have their sphere of influence reduced because they are unable to throw away their fear. Such people are so self-conscious they are afraid to be seen and heard. They are often overwhelmed in groups, inept in providing solutions to problems, and shy away from challenges.

If such is your problem, you will not set any goals and will be helpless in finding solutions to your day-to-day problems. David Allyn says, "When we are self-conscious, we become ineffective. We easily get trapped in a spiral of shame and embarrassment. The spiral can grow and grow until it wreaks havoc on our personal or professional relationships."[14]

Going by what Allyn is saying, you need to overcome this spiral of shame so that you can become productive. Do not succumb to your fears and yield

---

14. Allyn, David. *I Can't Believe I Just Did That: How (Seemingly) Small Embarrassments Can Wreak Havoc in Your Life—and What You Can Do to Put a Stop to Them.* New York: Penguin Group Inc., 2004, 4.

to situations that pose any challenges. Remember that if you continue to avoid challenging situations and interactions, you will build a cage for yourself, which you might mistakenly think will keep you safe. That is a sure way to become trapped in your small world.

GOD, EVER PRESENT, EVER HELPFUL

If you are a child of God, you need not be afraid because God is for you and so nothing can be against you. God is never absent from your life. He is always available to help you in your time of need. Remember this is the same God who did not spare his own Son but gave him up for you.

The good news is that no one can bring an accusation against you because God has already in Christ justified you. Christ did not only die but rose again from the dead and gave you victory. From this day onwards, acknowledge the mighty work of God on your behalf and do not give in to fear.

Let us look at another story to help you dispel any fears you may still have. A woman and her daughter were traveling cross-country by train. The child was enjoying the scenic beauty as she peeped into the window and made admiring comments.

Suddenly, she saw ahead of them a big river. Overwhelmed by fear she shouted to her mother. "Mother! Mother! We are going to fall into a river and die." But once they reached the river, there was a bridge that took them to the other side of the river. She settled down after that frightful experience to enjoy the scene once again. Then suddenly, without any warning, she saw a tall mountain ahead of them.

Again, overcome with fear, she shouted, "Mother! Mother! We are going to crash into the mountain and die." But when they reached the mountain, a tunnel carried them through it. On the other side, heaving a sigh of relief, she remarked. "Oh, Mother, someone has gone ahead of us to prepare the way." This might only be a story, but very often that is our approach to life. We react fearfully to any situation we cannot explain. However, there is a solution for how to deal with such circumstances: it is to put your trust in God and to have the belief in yourself to overcome. This way, you will never be fearful again.

When Israel left Egypt, they wandered in the desert for many years. Eventually, the leader who led them from Egypt himself died. Faced with an uncertain future, the people might have been fearful without measure. However, God was with them. He gave them a new leader in Joshua. God knew the people's apprehensions. Therefore, he instructed Joshua to let the priest carrying the Ark of God take the lead so that the people would follow.

That is the key to overcoming fear. Trust all your ways into the hands of God, and you will no longer be afraid to live. The prophet Isaiah had his ministry at a time when Israel was at a crossroad in their history. They had been under bondage from foreign nations. It was a period when they were under severe stress. God sent the prophet to tell them about their imminent and total deliverance from bondage.

His message dealt with negative and crippling fear. The type that can keep you from realizing your dreams. Israel's fears were the aftermath of oppression suffered through servitude to the Egyptians. Though the captivity was over, some of them still felt like they were captives.

The example of Israel shows that people who were once enslaved may still feel shackled even though they have gained their freedom. For all those who have been affected in any way by the evils of the slave trade, it is time to let go so that you can fulfill your true destiny.

The message that God gave to Israel through the prophet Isaiah still resonates today. Then and now, God assures us of his unwavering support even in times of our greatest needs, comparable to wading through waters or blazing through fires.

Although the hardships these extreme events could pose could be severe, God's intervention mitigates their threat. Above all, God constantly affirms our preeminence in his sight, warranting his relentless and assured protection.

There are people who have the premonition of something bad happening to them. They fear that they will catch the next dreadful disease in town, or they will be involved in an accident that will kill them or somebody related to them.

The biblical character Job was one such person. Whenever any of his children went out, he would offer sacrifices on their behalf, in case they did something bad. Eventually, he was afflicted with a serious case of disaster upon disaster. Finally, he could exclaim, "What I feared has come upon me; what I dreaded has happened to me" (Job 3:25).

Job willed calamity upon himself through his constant hunch of disaster. Instead of anticipating something bad happening to you, appropriate God's word that assures of his goodness and love following you all the days of your life and telling you that you will dwell in the house of the Lord forever.

For some of us, this message from God is too hard for us to digest. We are like Vera, a one-time neighbor of mine. She was always afraid that something terrible was going to happen to her or a member of her family. She would sit in tentacles when her husband had not returned from work or when her children had not returned from school.

One afternoon as she waited for her children to return from school, she heard that a school bus was involved in an accident with possibly one fatality and several injuries. With deep remorse, she wailed and rolled herself on the ground, crying for her son.

As she rolled on the ground, somebody who had been to the scene of the accident came and told her. "Women sit up; it was not your son's school bus." Several of us are like that. Whenever we hear of trouble, we see it at our doorsteps. We have the victim mentality. If you are such a person, the earlier you shirk that identity and take on that of a victor, the better.

PRACTICAL STEPS TO OVERCOMING FEAR

In his letter to the Philippians, Paul wrote: "Do not be anxious about anything, but in everything by prayer and supplication with thanksgiving let your requests be made known to God. And the peace of God, which surpasses all understanding, will guard your hearts and your minds in Christ Jesus" (Philippians 4:6-7).

As the apostle counseled, there are practical steps you can take to overcome fear in your life. This should begin with the cultivation of a never-give-up attitude. Such an approach does not ignore the existence of problems and challenges. Rather, it does not elevate fear and accord it powers it does not have.

Next, look for feasible ways to find solutions to problems as they arrive. For example, when you make appointments, be punctual. If you must make a speech, stick to the facts, and avoid the bent to embellish your speech to appear to others as sophisticated. People might see through the façade and lower the premium they put on you. Keep your conversations rich by mastering different subjects.

Likewise, make it a point to keep your word to earn credibility. When others find you authentic, it will give you the confidence you need to live life without pretense. Moreover, learn to live in the present and not be preoccupied with the future. The next day or year will find its solutions to problems when they arrive.

If your fear is shyness in front of other people, you must know that the next person might be as fearful as you are. You are all like little children in the playground. Allow yourself to flow freely, and you will find that others are as welcoming and helpful. If yours is anxiety regarding your future, take steps to put some changes in place. If you need to cut down on your expenses to put some savings aside, do it and stop being fearful. Always cure fear with action, and you will not succumb to the power that fear has over you.

FROM FEAR TO BOLDNESS

If you can follow the practical steps to overcome fear, you can regain your confidence to help you move from fear to boldness and self-assurance, and from failure to success. No longer will you allow fear to control who you are and what you can do. Just like how some people have managed to move from cowardice to bravery and from fearful to fearless, you too can move from zero to awesome and from nonentity to a Superstar.

This step can happen, but it will require the uttermost discipline as well as the ability to subject yourself to a set routine or new ways of doing things. You will need discipline and wisdom to help you stay focused on a goal.

Moreover, you need to fall in love with whatever task you perform to attain your set goal. Above all else, maintain uprightness in all you do or pursue. Do not approach any venture or event in your life with fear. Maintain a calm head in all circumstances so that you can think and devise ways to assail evil in your life. Likewise, yield your desires and undertakings to the creator who has big dreams for you. Next, ignite your inner strength so that you will not be passive in your fight against fear. It will help keep evil and misfortunes at bay.

CHAPTER FIVE
STOP WORRYING, IT'S A NUISANCE

*"Worry does not empty tomorrow of its sorrow,
it empties today of its strength."*
Corrie ten Boom

A STATE OF WORRY

Bianca and her husband lived in the Denver neighborhood of Westwood, a part of town that had seen a lot of trouble lately. There had been many burglaries and a drive by shooting episode. These incidents had left her fearful and worried about her family's prospects. She and her husband had plans to sell their house and relocate to a more peaceful neighborhood.

Meanwhile, they had to get a buyer for their house so that they could raise the money for the down payment for the new house. As they waited, Bianca continued to worry.

If she had to leave the house, she would check and double-check to make sure the doors were properly bolted. If her children had not returned from school, she would be full of uncertainties and doubt. She was afraid that they might accidentally be hit by a stray bullet from a drive-by shooting, even though she had only seen a single incident.

Her husband, seeing the strain she was under because of the troubles in their community counseled her to calm her nerves and trust everything into the hands of the Almighty God. But that was easier said than done.

Soon she began to experience migraines. When she visited her family doctor, he noticed the change in her health and advised her to reduce the stress otherwise she could suffer a stroke. The aftermath of all the fear that Bianca harbored brought on this chronic state of worry and uneasiness.

No doubt, she found herself in her present state because she allowed fear to cloud her judgment. Above all, the continued state of fear she experienced did not give her the time to examine her emotional well-being. Since Bianca was always on tenterhooks, she became impassive of what was going on around her.

Like Bianca, many of us likewise experience this state in our lives. Invariably, if we allow this behavior to go unchecked it can culminate in a pattern of chronic worry. The result for anyone in this state is to lose their sense of urgency, dampening any desire to strive to succeed in life.

Wayne Dyer claims that "People driven by intention are described as having a strong will that won't permit anything to interfere with achieving their inner desire."[15] Therefore, per this claim, if a person worries incessantly, it takes the place of purpose. It means that everything you do is led by worry and not intention. For that reason, you cannot achieve anything substantial in your life because worry has taken over any drive you have.

REASONS WHY PEOPLE WORRY

Every human being can be prone to worry. Though some worry more than others. Some people easily overcome setbacks and get on with their lives. Others, like Bianca, however, do not easily overcome what it is that is nagging them.

There are many reasons why people worry. As we saw with Bianca, mothers usually worry about the safety of their families. For some people, it is the fear of getting a disease and not being able to meet their needs let alone those of their families.

If you are a child, you worry whether your parents are going to be around to meet your needs. There are those who worry about when and who to marry.

---

15. Dyer, Wayne W. *The Power of Intention: Learning to Co-create Your World Your Way*. Carlsbad, California: Hay House Inc., 2004, 3.

For those who are already married, there is the nagging issue of whether they will meet the needs of their spouse. Occasionally there is the suspicion of whether their spouses are being faithful to them.

Most often, for parents, their worry is about their children. A famous example is the biblical character, Job. He was so embroidered with worry for his children that he always performed sacrifices to atone for their inadvertent sins.

Some of us also worry about money. We are so preoccupied with how much money we make and how that will suffice to pay for our numerous bills. Yet, there are those whose prime cause for worry is death. This group is fearful of making a wrong move at any time and thus stepping into the trap of death.

Then some worry about what other people think of them. Therefore, they are unable to stand on their own two feet. They are always seeking approval before they undertake any venture in life. Sometimes, a person's cause of worry comes from the family she is born into or the friends she associates with. Sometimes these associations seem to impede one's forward march and so tend to become a source of worry.

THE LEADING CAUSE OF PEOPLE'S WORRY

The source of most people's worries is chronic anticipation of negative events. They anticipate running into unexpected problems such as disease, spousal infidelity, or even death. These premonitions unchecked sprout into real problems that cause material harm to victims. Whilst most individuals' hunches center on the daily woes of life, some incessantly have instincts of something bad happening to them.

A person whose actions fit the above was Keisha, a single mother who lived in a low-income housing community in Globeville, Denver, with her two sons. Her sons were five years apart, so they attended separate schools close to her house. Every day she would go out to watch her boys go to school.

Caring for those boys without the help of a spouse had made Keisha very sensitive. She always worried unduly about her boys, particularly when they left the house to go to school or play outside with friends. Even when they were at school, she continuously worried about them. Whenever she heard something bad happened in a school, she would run to each of her sons' schools to check on them.

One day whilst her sons were at school, she received a phone call from her eldest son's school informing her the school was on lockdown. The message was informing parents that despite the lockdown, everything was under control, so no one should worry.

Unfortunately for Keisha, she did not listen to the entire message. Instead, she became hysterical and, in the process, had a massive heart attack. Neighbors made a 911 call for her. Fortunately, an ambulance was promptly dispatched to her. However, the extent of the heart attack was so severe she stayed in a coma at the ICU for three days. Despite the good work of the medics, on the third day, she passed away.

Several people are like Keisha. They are always expecting trouble because of their worry pattern. Unfortunately for Keisha, there was no second chance. However, you still have the chance to resolve your problem of worry. The warning here is that if your worry pattern is like that of Keisha or Bianca, you are sitting on a volcano that can erupt at any time.

Therefore, recognize that shortfall and deal with it before things turn out for the worse. The fact is, unless you act fast and find a solution to this worry problem you would be in for a rude awakening. Interestingly, your worrying about things will not change the facts; therefore, eschew all tendency to worry and just allow the liquid to find its level.

THE NEGATIVE EFFECTS OF WORRY

Worry, like its counterpart fear, is a nuisance that can also have a devastating effect on human effort. While fear can have a crippling effect, worry can even be more debilitating, reducing a functioning individual to an imbecile unable to operate normally in society. If you suffer from such an illness, you will come short in any project. Even simple acts such as getting out of the house to run errands or to go to work can become daunting. For such a chronic worrier, your world is one of limitless troubles and misfortunes. This self-caused misfortune, therefore, will keep you from realizing your dreams and achieving your fullest potential.

However, in life, you cannot be careful enough because it does not matter how well you make your plans; there could always be a hitch somewhere. There is not an individual on earth who would never make mistakes or get into some form of trouble at one time or another.

The best indicator of what worry can cause was what happened to the New York Stock Exchange and other major international markets after the terrorist attack of September 11, 2001. On that day, in a series of coordinated attacks suicide bombers belonging to the Islamic terrorist group al-Qaeda flew planes into the World Trade Center in New York, and the Pentagon in Arlington County.

A third plane intended for the White House crashed in a field near Shanksville, Pennsylvania when passengers on the plane confronted the hijackers. To say these attacks caused a significant economic impact on the United States and world markets is an understatement.

When the attacks happened, the stock exchanges stayed closed until September 17. When finally, it reopened, the Dow Jones Industrial Average (DJIA) fell 684 points, 7.1%, to 8921, a record-setting one-day point decline. This decline was to continue so that at the week's end, the Dow Jones had fallen 1,369.7 points (14.3%). To this day, that trend has been the largest one-week point drop in history. When calculated in 2001-dollar values, the U.S. stocks lost $1.4 trillion in valuation for the week.

The tragic fall in the value of the stock market cannot be attributed to anything the Exchange did or did not do. The simple cause was anxiety generated by the attack. Many people were worried enough to get out of their houses. Coupled with these, many investors were "panic selling," thinking the world was coming to an end. Like the trend of the markets, if we worry, it tends to have adverse effects on anything we do. It can stall all our efforts and cause us to flounder in any undertaking.

REASONS WHY YOU SHOULD NOT WORRY

With hindsight, the trend the market followed is seen as something that should not have happened. The reason is that the precautions the US government took ensured that the terrorists were never able to come back to cause further devastation. This means that, often our hunches of evil are not likely to be realized.

If we can discover why worry is unnecessary, it would be good to turn to the teachings of Jesus. In his Sermon on the Mount, Jesus touched on the topic of worry. He charged his listeners not to be anxious about their lives, as to what they will eat or what they will drink.

Jesus also told his listeners not to worry about clothing or shelter because the life they possessed was comparatively more valuable. He contended that their creator cared about them. God cares about the birds of the sky and fish in the sea. Humans, Jesus alluded, were more valuable, so we should be aware that God was not going to allow us to go without the basic needs of life.

There are certain things you cannot run from as a human being. Whilst you are alive, you must pay your bills if you do not want to be thrown out of your house or apartment. Besides that, you should be aware that if you are going to buy things, you must pay taxes. In that vein, you do not worry and complain about paying all the taxes, because your complaints will not stop you from paying those taxes.

Therefore, simply do what you are supposed to do to get those out of the way. Finally, because you are a human being, you will eventually die, so you don't have to be all fearful about dying because it is inescapable. When your time comes, you will go. Therefore, make the best of your life so that when the time comes for you to go, there will be no regrets.

Besides these, you will be disappointed by the people you love and put your trust in. When that happens, recognize that they are human, and so can err. You can become sick, lose a job, or even experience the death of a loved one. All these are things you should anticipate so that when they happen, you do not become all worked up.

DEAL WITH YOUR PATTERN OF WORRY

If you are unable to overcome your bent for worrying you will continually be an underachiever. The reason is that a pattern of worry can lead you to have a false sense of security in daydreaming as a way of escaping reality.

Unfortunately, anyone who falls victim to daydreaming experiences the adverse effect of impairment in their ability to do anything meaningful. In the final analysis, all daydreaming does is continue to make the victim experience the fantasy world with no real idea of how to tackle the many challenges life throws at him. That person becomes like the ostrich that buries its head in the sand instead of making bold strides to get their life into gear.

If your worry pattern can be traced to your associations, you must come to a moment of truth. As an individual, you cannot discount your family or friends, so study how you can develop better relationships with them. Truth be told, every one of us was born into a family and a country. We, therefore, have a past associated with us. Whether you like where you were born or not, whether you like your family or not, you cannot change it. If your friends and family had caused you any pain in the past, ignoring them or running away from them would not solve any of your problems. What would help you would be to find them out and settle whatever differences you have.

For some people, the cause of their worry is marriage and relationships. They might have felt cheated or taken advantage of in the past, such that they closed the door to any future relationships. In their opinion, marriage is not worth pursuing because of all the pain that is presumably associated with it. If you find yourself in such a group, you must accept that what has happened has happened. You cannot change it; what you can change is to take bold steps to begin things anew. Otherwise, you would continue to brood and wallow in self-pity. In the end, the one who gets hurt is you.

As you worry your body gradually wastes away. This is because your pattern of worry weakens your immune system, breaking down your body's ability to fight external threats. For that reason, you make yourself vulnerable to diseases and infections. The opposite is also true. A worry-free person has a strong and effective immune system because his senses are always alerted to ward off any invaders.

Psalm 127, a Song of Ascents attributed to Solomon, makes it plain that though people put in hard work to erect structures for a city, its true builder is God. Similarly, though people may put security measures in place, the provider of protection is no other than God.

This Psalm displays the futility of worry and anxiety. It shows that anxiety has zero positive effects on the accomplishment of any venture. On the other hand, unbridled worry can stem the progress of any undertaking. In that vein, the earlier you deal with your pattern of worry the better it will be for you.

GOD'S PROVIDENCE EASES ALL WORRY

You see, your Father in heaven knows every need of yours. He takes care of all your needs. His assurance is that his goodness and mercy will follow you all the days of your life. Even when you are in the narrowest of corners, he will sustain you. So, don't freak out, because help is always available to you.

Besides, you cannot avert trouble by worrying because what will happen will happen. Moreover, as a believer, you must know that your God is in control, and he deals with your daily problems as they arise. You may not recognize it, but no human power can be compared to that of God. When he takes charge of your life, nothing out of the ordinary can happen to you.

Each passing day is sure to bring its challenges, but since God is on top of things, it should give us cause to refrain from worrying, knowing that no matter how big a problem is, he has a solution at hand. Every day God throws an open invitation to us to come to the source of relief. This call is open to everyone and is without a price. Therefore, we should avail ourselves of this open invitation and come before his throne of grace to cast all our cares upon him.

STEPS TO CUT DOWN WORRY

Admittedly, there is no one-size-fits-all solution for the problem of worry. Neither can anyone solve their problems by being anxious. What a person can do is put in measures that will reduce stress levels and help her take charge of situations.

The key to stemming any pattern of worry in your life is to realize that you need to put a stop to the habit. Having done that, you must resolve to take steps that will eliminate the condition permanently. Know that without a purposeful resolve, you cannot achieve anything meaningful.

Therefore, determine intentionally to stop any pattern of worry before it blossoms into something big and uncontrollable. To do this, you will need the discipline to subject yourself to a set routine, and the tenacity to stay focused on your set goal. If your source of worry is about not making enough money, take measures that can stem the dearth of cash flow, such as changing jobs or getting a second job.

Sometimes, it is not simply the question of not making enough money, but it is an inability to properly plan how you spend your money. Hence, stem this tide by watching your spending habits. Have a plan in place for paying your debts, such as credit cards and car loans, among others.

The secret is that if you pay your bills on time, it will help you with your credit score. That improved credit score is more than money in your pocket because it is going to help you pay for things with a lower interest rate.

For some of us, our financial woes stem from the fact that we follow the fashion trend. We desire to acquire the latest gadget, or the latest car, or dress trending. All these contribute to hurting our bottom line. However, as a sign of maturity, you cannot live simply to fulfill any nagging desire you have. Learn to exercise self-control so that you do not unnecessarily burden yourself.

Sometimes you might look at your circumstances and begin to worry because you falsely conclude that you are the only one singled out by providence to undergo trials and temptations. But you are not alone. Every person born of a woman undergoes suffering, albeit at a different degree. Yours might even be lighter than another person's.

Therefore, don't bemoan your misfortunes and get crippled from carrying on with the business of life. The act of worrying does not come out of the blue. Rather it is a habit that is cultivated over a long period. Worry is like a weed. If you do not uproot a weed from its source, it will germinate right after it has been cut down. So, similarly, tackle all worry and anxiety at its source. When all is done, do not discount physical exercises because they could help you release the tension that has built up in your muscles.

WHERE TO FIND LASTING PEACE

Many of us worry because we are consumed with the cares of this life. As believers, we do not seek to go along with anything the world desires, but we strive at any time to present our bodies pure and preserved. In that way, our worship of God becomes more meaningful, because we recognize that there is no peace in merely acquiring stuff. True peace comes from trusting God to take us through life, one day at a time.

Jesus, in his many discourses, showed that when you allow God's word into your heart, you will find peace. An instance of this was when he was invited to the house of a rich benefactor called Martha in the village of Bethany in Judea. Martha, the wealthy woman, lived with her brother Lazarus and sister Mary. Whilst Martha was busy preparing dinner, her sister was sitting at the feet of Jesus listening to God's word. Martha, who in every way was overwhelmed with the preparations, complained to Jesus about her sister, who was not offering her any assistance.

To the surprise of Martha and those gathered there, Jesus reprimanded Martha for complaining instead of advising Mary to play her role as co-host. Jesus' response showed that true peace comes from knowing God's word. Many of us worry because we fail to recognize that if we know our God things will always work out for us, even if they do not happen in the way we prefer. God knows best what we need. That always becomes evident if we are unwavering in our faith because God does not renege on his promises.

No matter how cornered we think we are, our God will always meet our needs. Above all, let this new direction you are taking guide you into scaling heights you never dreamt about, all the time yielding to God's final authority in all your endeavors.

One good way to reduce stress is to meditate on the word of God. Anyone who concentrates his or her thinking on God is indeed kept in perfect peace. Notably, the prophet Isaiah wrote: "Thou wilt keep him in perfect peace, whose mind is stayed on thee: because he trusteth in thee" (Isaiah 26:3 KJV).

God's word explicitly asks the believer to cast his cares and anxieties on God. He is implored to let God do all caring which he alone is capable of. Writing to the Macedonian Christians, Paul asked them: "Do not be anxious about anything, but in everything by prayer and supplication with thanksgiving let your requests be made known to God. And the peace of God, which surpasses all understanding, will guard your hearts and your minds in Christ Jesus" (Philippians 4:6-7).

As a believer, you should always be comforted by the fact that only the Lord Jesus gives true peace. In that vein, if you are constantly focused on God there is every indication that you will have perfect peace. The Psalmist said he had hidden God's word in his heart so that it would help him to overcome the temptation to sin. When you meditate on God's word, your focus in life will change from things that are transient to those that guarantee lasting satisfaction.

Whenever you are tempted to yield to anxiety, you should recognize that Christ's work has taken away any reproach that you had. Therefore, you no longer face censorship and condemnation for your past actions. You are no longer subject to a long list of dos and don'ts. Rather, your life has been freed from any hold which the devil had on you. Have renewed hope for life. Get out of the dark and shady places. Let the sun shine on you and brighten your path. You are a victor, so cease acting as a victim, because there is nothing out there to get you.

CHAPTER SIX

ENTHUSIASM HAS POSITIVE EFFECTS

"The secret of genius is to carry the spirit of the child into old age, which means never losing your enthusiasm."
Aldous Huxley

WHAT IS ENTHUSIASM?

One day at our church board meeting we were all in a somber mood because things were not working as they should. I had mooted an idea that had taken me days to ponder over. Before coming to this meeting, I had considered the pros and cons and perceived that we stood to benefit by adopting it. However, the other members of the board would not have anything to do with it.

When I thought the idea was defeated and I was about to give up, one member, Lewis, who was always bursting with enthusiasm, took up an advocacy role and vehemently defended the proposal. Thoughtfully, he laid down the pros and cons just as I had arrived at in my planning. Instantly, as if he had waved a magic wand, all the members who were initially pessimistic and were arguing fervently against the idea saw what a good notion it was.

The members were won over by Lewis who enthusiastically endorsed the idea and put up a good argument on what a great opportunity we would be passing by voting against it. Like Lewis, you can make gains if others see the way you display passion and enthusiasm in all of life's endeavors. This notion was reinforced by the development at our meeting.

It opened my eyes to see how much any person can accomplish if their enthusiasm levels are high. Truly, enthusiastic people are the real Superstars around. For in their enthusiasm, they carry all the others with them. Consequently, if your life has come to a standstill, if you see no way forward, try enthusiasm. It will help you banish the blues, whip up your interest, and keep you focused.

The power of enthusiasm, no doubt, will become more evident if we trace it to its roots. Our English word enthusiasm comes from two Greek words *en* (in) and *theos* (God). Thus, by inference, an enthusiastic person has the spirit of God within. Simply put, it is one in whom the spirit of God dwells. So, because the spirit of God indwells the enthusiastic person, he or she has a happy disposition.

Another way to describe enthusiasm is to say a person has an adrenaline rush. Adrenaline is a hormone which is secreted by the adrenal glands. When these hormones are released into the bloodstream, they spark hyperactivity. Such is the power enthusiasm possesses that if you gain an understanding of its workings, you can take your life to a different level. It will give you drive and passion and will make you attack life with appetite and feeling. Let us, therefore, look at how we can gain this dynamic force and how we can use it to make life joyous.

PERSONALITY TYPE AND ENTHUSIASM

Though many factors determine a person's enthusiasm level, one of the most important is the individual's temperament or Personality type. The broadest classification of temperament has two main divisions: introvert and extrovert. However, there is a further categorization into four main groups derived from the findings of the "father of medicine," the Greek physician *Hippocrates* (460-370 BC). He concluded that there were four main temperament types depending on various body fluids: "Blood,"; "choler," or "yellow bile,"; "melancholy," or "black bile," and "phlegm."

Though scientists have disproved any direct relations between body fluid and temperament, Hippocrates' designation of four main divisions, as well as the names, have stuck. The four groups are Sanguine, Choleric, Melancholic, and Phlegmatic. In later developments, these temperaments have also been described as *personality types*. The Corresponding Personality types are Expressive, Analytical, Amiable, and Driver. In this book, however, I shall use the personality types as they speak more relevantly to the common person on the street.

THE EXPRESSIVE PERSONALITY

The person with the Expressive Personality, also called the Sanguine, desires influence, and to be the center of attention. They have a pleasant and affable demeanor which contributes in no small measure to make them sociable, warm-hearted, and optimistic. Besides that attribute, they can be sincere at heart as they can be creative and colorful.

Moreover, they possess the spirit of a child and are full of energy and enthusiasm. This group cannot be said to be self-righteous; they simply do not have time to brood over mishaps and past performance, and neither do they bear grudges. This child-like attitude on their part makes them receptive to religion and what it has to offer. Their outlook on life affects the way they see and react to anything in their life. Presumably, they have limited knowledge of human shortfalls and worldly matters.

Consequently, due partly to their perception of the world, they sometimes exhibit a childlike naivety in their approach to life. On the positive side, there is not a slight hint of pessimism in them. Instead, they are exuberant, vibrant, and alive. As an added feature to their affable nature, they have a special interest in nature; an interest which becomes one of their main incentives for living.

Consequently, they do not stay indoors and keep to themselves, but they saunter outdoors, appreciating everything—trees, flowers, birds, among others. As a bonus, their cheerful and outgoing personalities predispose them towards passionate enthusiasm.

THE DRIVER PERSONALITY

The Driver Personality, sometimes described as the Choleric temperament, is a fact-based extrovert who is primarily ruthlessly determined and ambitious. Not only are they born leaders, but they are often hard-driving individuals. They can be uncompromising and self-conceited.

Their dominant personalities make them desire control and authority. This attribute make them function best at jobs that do not only require strong control and authority but also require swift decision-making and prompt attention. The Driver Personality, being fact-driven, cares little about sentiments.

A major strength of this type of personality is leadership ability. He or she always exudes confidence, the confidence of a strong-willed but naturally gifted individual who is self-sufficient and thrives on opposition. Though the Driver Personality is much more prone to mood swings, they are in no way low on enthusiasm.

THE AMIABLE PERSONALITY

The Amiable Personality, also called the Phlegmatic, is a relationship introvert who has a relaxed and quiet demeanor. He or she can be warm and at the same time, slothful and inactive. Their relational and amiable qualities allow this personality type to perform best in mediating conflicts and restoring unity. If the situation requires steadiness as well as the calmness needed to calm matters, they provide a solid front to bring situations under control.

The Phlegmatic tends to be easygoing, content with self, calm, cool and collected, tolerant of others, and very well-balanced. Notwithstanding, such people can be indecisive and chronic worriers. This demeanor will make the amiable phlegmatic low on enthusiasm.

Furthermore, they are fearful and indecisive and tend to have a compromising nature. Because they are interested in cooperation and interpersonal harmony, it tends to make them over-concerned with other people. Such posture contributes to reducing their enthusiasm levels significantly. Although

Amiable Personalities are very empathetic, they can be selfish, judgmental, and passively aggressive. This way, they not only dampen their enthusiasm but also that of those around them.

THE ANALYTICAL PERSONALITY

The Analytical Personality, or the Melancholic temperament, is a fact-based introvert and is characterized by thoughtfulness and attentiveness. The term Melancholic, though, is a misnomer since it fails to emphasize the analytical strengths of such people.

Their personality type make them move with caution and restraint in any and every one of life's undertakings. They are best at attending to details as well as analyzing problems. They also tend to be deep-thinkers and feelers who often see the negative attributes of life, rather than the good and positive things. Their perfectionist outlook on life make them low on enthusiasm.

Seldom does one see them expressly happy. Instead, what is seen by others are individuals who are often lonely and deserted. Sadly, many Analytical Personalities are also victims of deep bouts of depression that come from great dissatisfaction, disappointment, and hurtful words or events. Analytical Personalities are people who have a deep love for others, while usually holding themselves in contempt. In short, they take life very seriously, and it often leaves them feeling blue, helpless, or even hopeless.

THE ROLE OF PERSONALITY TYPE, AND THEN SOME

As an individual, you are defined, among other things, by your Personality Type. However, the good news is that no individual displays wholly one trait. Any one person can possess aspects of all four types. Nevertheless, there is usually one type that stands out. Your level of enthusiasm is usually determined by the predominant type of personality trait you possess. However, enthusiasm is stimulated by the self.

If you are a person who is always thinking about yourself, no matter your personality type, you will not be enthused about many things. As Ed Young says, if we are a people who are self-absolved, we possess a kind "of preoccupation with self [which] prevents us from connecting with others."[16]

Besides your personality type, your attitude can also determine your level of enthusiasm. If you are an individual who turns trivial and insignificant ills into tribulations, if you are prone to a morbid outlook on life, and if you tend to maximize evil, you will not be enthusiastic.

Yet another determinant of your behavior as a human being is the interplay of the conscious and the subconscious. The subconscious harbors our moments of excitement as well as sadness, a traumatic and harrowing experience, or one of contentment and healing. Sometimes our traumatic experiences come to the fore and haunt us. These traumatic experiences can greatly dampen any person's enthusiasm.

THE MISERY-HAPPINESS LINE

The role of these personality types in determining each person's level of enthusiasm is very significant, but so are the other factors. Though, as individuals, we do not all have the same enthusiasm levels, there should be a striving on the part of any person desiring to conquer life to attempt to become their best.

A good way to measure your enthusiasm level is to find your position on an imaginary line which will tell you where you are in your level of development. This imaginary line, the misery-happiness line, will help you find where you are in this quest. Ideally, the extrovert will be placed above this line, while the introvert will be placed below it. The rationale for this placement is that extroverts do not harbor any ill feelings. Added to this, they are always livid with enthusiasm, so they earn a place at the top of the line.

On the other hand, introverted personalities are measured downward of this line because their trademark is gloom and pessimism. This said, however,

---

16. Young, Ed. *Outrageous, Contagious Joy: Five Big Questions to Help You Discover One Great Life*. New York: The Berkley Publishing Group, 2007, 136.

it is hardly the case that any one personality type is fixed in position relative to this line. This is so because individuals can exhibit different traits at any time of their lives.

Nevertheless, the place of a person on this divide does not make one perfect or imperfect. Because all human beings are flawed. What makes the difference is the spirit of God indwelling a person. Thus, all people have the hard task of struggling to stay up the misery-happiness line. This is so because an individual, assumed to be cheerful or moody, can have mood changes that will shift their position on the line.

Thus, while extroverts have the task of staying on top of the line, the mission of introverts is to move up the line. Once this threshold is reached, a level of equilibrium is established, and the enthusiasm that one needs for life becomes available. Such a state is only possible when you can control your thoughts and actions and strive for noble ideals.

THE CONTROLLED PERSONALITY

To reach the equilibrium on the Misery-Happiness line depends on how one exercises self-control and also allows the Holy Spirit to operate in their life. When you have self-control, you can determine what it is you want out of life. Your life is focused and intentional. You know what you want, and you go for it. On the other hand, when the Holy Spirit indwells you, it will show up in the fruit you bear. You will show love and will always be happy and peaceful. This joy that the Holy Spirit gives you makes you expressive so that it becomes evident to others the beauty you radiate.

The controlled personality you acquire will make you appear stable and unshakable because any erratic behavior will be uprooted from your life. Selfishness, bitterness, and fear can no longer truncate your life because you will be on top of your act. Also, it will enable you to shed all negative and depressive tendencies in your life and always take on a semblance of cheerfulness.

There are viable steps you can take despite your personality type to achieve a life that gives assurance to others and also screams confidence. This lifestyle should begin with the attainment of a life that does not recall mistakes and shortcomings.

Next, you should adopt a positive attitude where you see everything as good and pleasant. It is alright to show your despair and be exasperated but do not let that keep you down. If you must weep, please do, and do not bottle your grief but allow emotions to flow so that, in the process, you will receive healing and the motivation to stay enthusiastic. Subsequently, you should cultivate a healthful attitude whereby you will see goodness in everybody and every condition. Whilst at this, empower your thought process to portray to others a sense of fulfillment and cheerfulness.

At any time, let others feel a sense of happiness that will affirm to them a person who is clearly in charge. Likewise, be deliberate, and adopt an optimistic attitude that will enliven your life. This optimistic lifestyle can be cultivated intentionally by you and through the enabling of the Holy Spirit.

Also, adopt a mantra for your life. It is always good to figure out what you want and to put them in short memorable words which you can repeat to yourself at intervals. The repeated use of these affirmations will help you keep up your enthusiasm and zeal for living. What these declarations will do for you will be to curb fear and help you build confidence in your abilities.

DEPRESSION AND ENTHUSIASM

When you develop a control personality, you acquire a near invincibility. However, there is one enemy—depression that can fight against your ability to always exercise a controlled life and stay enthusiastic. You see, feelings of pessimism and despair about your prospects in life are normal. However, if not controlled, they can give you a sense of fear in your ability to accomplish anything worthwhile.

Usually, your state of mind and well-being determine how strong or weak you are. If you are strong, you can survive adversity, but if you are weak, you can easily give in to depression. Weak people, often unable to bear the load of their suffering, are more liable to give in to negative actions such as suicide, drunkenness, and drug abuse.

The strong-minded person, however, comes out of such situations strengthened to carry on with the business of daily living. They admit that life has a way of giving us the hard blows. They also recognize that it can pose challenges that not only overwhelm us and make us morbidly melancholic but can also affect our enthusiasm.

On a personal level, acknowledge that challenges will come. Then, when they happen, you must be realistic and understand that those sad feelings relate directly to the side of you, which is prone to negativity and hopelessness.

Besides that, there should be the recognition that all people are subject to mood changes. Therefore, each person should have in place mechanisms by which he can get out of an uncomfortable situation. You have to act according to how you want to feel, and it will usually happen accordingly.

William James asserts: "Believe that life is worth living, and your belief will help you create the fact."[17] This attitude will grant you the force that will counteract your pessimism. You must understand this from your thinking that no state is static. Furthermore, you must always believe that living things are endowed with the ability to change their circumstances. Armed with this belief, anybody can get out of his or her sunken state.

STEPS TO OVERCOME DEPRESSION AND STAY ENTHUSIASTIC

Since depression can sap all your energy and leave you with a feeling of despair and gloom, it can become your greatest enemy if you allow it to fester. Due to its distressing effect, you should not give it any room to dominate your life and quash any happiness you may have.

The good news is that depression can be conquered with enthusiastic fervor and an adoption of a positive attitude. Bear in mind that to fight depression, you need to take some practical steps. These steps should begin with your belief in the goodness of God and the abundance he makes available. You should hold on to unwavering faith and a belief in your abilities. Take control of your life and overcome the bouts of shame that sometimes

---

17. James, William. The Will to Believe and Other essays in popular philosophy. New York, Dover Publications, INC. 1956.62

seem to overpower you and prevent you from taking concrete action to better yourself.

Furthermore, pursue faith in God because it could endow you with selfless abilities, which, in the long run, will give you an enthusiasm for living. Moreover, set times aside for daily morning devotions and Bible study. Such a practice will help you focus on God instead of your problems.

Additionally, your ability to hold on to positive thoughts and empowerment will always keep you enthusiastic. Hold on to a joyous mindset that cannot be dimmed by the problems of the day. Whenever a negative thought comes into your mind, replace it with that which is affirmative and uplifting.

Moreover, you need to clear your mind of things that have been overshadowing you and keeping your spirits low. You must intentionally determine to stay optimistic even when there is nothing to stay optimistic for. As much as you can, free your thoughts of all negativities. Get over difficult situations by sprinkling your life with laughter. A smile has a way of lighting your spirits. The magic laughter performs is to take any load from your mind, thus helping you relieve stress.

If you give in to sad thoughts, you will be sad; on the other hand, if you entertain happy thoughts, you will be happy and enthusiastic about life. Our thoughts primarily go to make us the people we are. So, whenever you see the depressive mood coming, kick yourself into action and strive to stay on the positive side.

This will also depend on how you use your subconscious mind. Develop the habit of making repeated suggestions to it: when you wake up in the morning, throughout the day, and more especially before falling asleep in the night. This repeated use of suggestions will help change the way you think and thereby help you stay enthusiastic.

Ordinarily, a religious person has more enthusiasm in life than a person without God. His enthusiasm comes from the power and inspiration that he derives from prayer, prophecy, and the inspiration he gets daily from being associated with God.

The once impracticable person gains visionary experiences through his or her association with God and becomes motivated into a person of action and achievement. Such a renewed posture underscores the importance of religion to psychologically psyche a person up to gain confidence and discipline for life.

Likewise, focus on the here and now. Avoid thinking about what you missed or forfeited, or what you could have been. While those things you missed may not come back, they could be replaced with those that have even more potential.

Again, be self-disciplined and cultivate a tendency toward self-determination. At the same time, be confident in your ability without necessarily being unduly aggressive. Be a responsible member of the society in which you live by readily accepting leadership roles and striving to make meaningful contributions to that society.

Furthermore, avoid speaking pejoratively of others regardless of their nationality, class, occupation, or any period of the world's history in which they are situated. Besides these, seek out good friends in whose company you can always feel accepted and loved. This aside, you should also seek to help others who are in similar situations or even worse than you, and you will see the fulfillment that comes from knowing that you have been of help to another human being.

If you can follow these basic rules, you will avoid the sporadic blues and maintain an optimism driven by adventurism and a pioneering spirit. You will stay enthusiastic, and the occasional challenges of life will never dim your light.

CHAPTER SEVEN

HOLD ON TO UNDYING HOPE IT WILL SUSTAIN YOU

"Three grand essentials to happiness in this life are something to do, something to love and something to hope for."
Joseph Addison

WAIT AND HOPE

Lux and Greg lived in a studio apartment in Draper, Salt Lake City. They were not a married couple, just friends. Lux had been married three times already and loathed the idea of going into another marriage. Greg, a veteran, hurt himself in his last tour of duty and came home as an invalid.

For a few months after he returned from the war, his wife welcomed him with open arms. But Greg was not the same man he was before going to war. He was suffering from PTSD and frequently underwent mood changes. After a few months, his wife gave up on him, so he moved in with Lux.

I happened to be introduced to Lux and Greg by a friend of theirs. When I met them, they were already drinking too much alcohol. I counseled them to moderate their drinking, but all my advice fell on deaf ears.

Six months after I met them, Greg died. The autopsy showed that his liver was damaged through excessive drinking. I used Greg's death as an object lesson for Lux, but she admitted to me that there was nothing to live for. The last time I saw her, she was her usual drunk self. People like Lux, amid all the troubles they have encountered, have given up on life. Consequently, they do not care about what they take into their bodies. If your life has relapsed like Lux's, I want to entreat you to hang in there.

Alexander Dumas in his book, *The Count of Monte Cristo*, wrote: "Until the day when God shall deign [consent] to reveal the future to man, all human wisdom is summed up in these two words, -Wait and hope."[18] These words, wait and hope, are ancient wisdom that you could appeal to, to give direction to your life.

Waiting, is a line of action many people are uncomfortable to toll. Particularly if your life has taken a turn for the worst, like Lux, you may feel less motivated to wait, let alone entertain any hope. Hoping for a better future is not only for people who seem to have come to a dead end in their lives. Every human being on earth stands to benefit from hoping for a brighter and idyllic future.

Nevertheless, in our impatience, we allow our intolerance to morph into a malaise. However, when all hope seems lost, when you think, you have come to the end of your rope, waiting and hoping is the only thing that can keep you on course to attain superstar status.

THE MERITS OF WAITING

There are great merits in waiting because it can expose a lot of truth to you. Waiting can bring a lot of anguish, but if you prevail, it will not only make you strong but will also give you a survival instinct. That will, in turn, help develop strength in your character to make you steadfast in all you do.

In the 37th Psalm, the writer urges the upright person not to worry about dishonest people who prosper. He alleged that honest people may worry when they see errant ones prospering despite their assumed ill-discipline.

In today's *lingo*, we will say that the mischievous prosper because they are only concerned with their end goal and not the means to get there. Such people, he claimed, malign the honest who settle for what is untainted and ethical. The Psalmists warn that the great achievements of the dishonest notwithstanding, their ill-gotten gain will wither and tail off.

---

18. http://www.goodreads.com/author/quotes/4785.Alexandre_Dumas accessed April 11, 2015

The Psalmist's assertion about the upright showed the merits of waiting. He claimed that those who do not rush through projects achieve lasting results. This is possible because frank people seldom take the easy way out. They put a lot of planning into their work to make their achievements lasting. Thus, if you achieve lasting results for your efforts, it helps build your resume. Additionally, it helps you build trust. People will look at your achievements and entrust you with more responsibility.

Another merit of waiting is that when you work meticulously on a project, you can salivate the product. Likewise, if you wait for the right time to decide, you can weigh up the pros against the cons to come up with a good decision.

WAITING BUCKS TODAY'S TREND

Notwithstanding the merits of waiting, it bucks the trend in our world today. Though past generations had problems of waiting as we do today, we seem more inclined to impatience and rush to get things done now. It is this weakness that pushes people today to make rush decisions. We hardly make time to wait for any opportunity to come to us. We fail to wait for the right time to take up a job or embark on a venture.

We fail to realize that though decisiveness is good, patient maneuvering is even more ideal. That the benefits of testing the waters far outweigh any desire to plunge straight into it. Our generation of young people is the smartest we have seen over the ages.

Nevertheless, when they are saddled with the task of making major life decisions, they are found wanting. These areas include the choice of professions, friends, and life partners. The women are inclined to go to great lengths to secure a life partner when they feel that the prime of life is about to pass them.

They are unable to wait for the right time for their suitors. That said, every human being, both male and female, young and old, is not immune to impatience. The bare truth is that if we as humans can wait and hope, if we have patience and can wait for the right time, we will reap great rewards. In life, we can experience things, and we can hope for things. One incident can turn your life on its ears, while another can turn it upside down.

If you are married, there can be divorce; if you have a job, you could lose it. All such mishaps can happen to you. But what is important is how you deal with it. As Hewitt and co say, "When life knocks you to your knees, you're in a good position to pray."[19] The ability to prayerfully wait for your chance can become the greatest weapon you have in your arsenal. You should develop your ability to contemplate issues before you ever make any decisions in your life. Otherwise, you will make decisions which you will live to regret throughout your life.

DRAWBACKS OF IMPATIENCE

Though waiting has many merits, it is not always that we can do so. We become impatient because we want things to happen quickly. The biblical king Saul, the first king of Israel, was touted as the most qualified person to lead Israel in their time of uncertainty. However, later in his reign, he was disqualified because he could not wait for the prophet to come and pray before he went to war with his enemies.

Saul is not alone in this conduct. Many great leaders have been blighted by impatience. In 2002, after the terrorist attack in New York, President Bush of the US led a coalition to war with Iraq on the pretext that it possessed weapons of mass destruction. President Bush was supported by Tony Blair, the Prime Minister of Britain.

Later, it was found that the reason for going to war was a hoax. The fallout from this hastily taken decision was alarming. While President Bush managed to hang on to power, the British Prime Minister lost his position. Nonetheless, the former also lost his credibility with the two chambers of Congress and with the American public. The tragedy of the Iraqi war was that

---

19. Hewitt, Les & Charlie Self. *The Power of Faithful Focus: A Practical Christian Guide to Spiritual & Personal Abundance.* Deerfield Beach Florida: Faith Communication, Inc. 2004, 3.

these two world leaders failed to show the one trait essential for leadership: the ability to wait and weigh up matters before making any major decision.

When it comes to measuring the coping capacity of the human ability to wait, sometimes, children display the most impatience. My family usually prefer a home-cooked meal. Seldom do we go out for meals. Fortunately, my wife is one of the greatest cooks in the world.

Whether it is dumplings, chapatti (a Kenyan Indian dish), lasagna, or jollof rice (a Ghanaian dish), she is superb. Her menus range from European to American and a variety of African dishes. Not only is she a good cook but she is unusually fast when cooking.

One afternoon we all returned from church tired and hungry. As she usually does, my wife rushed to the kitchen to fix something for us to eat. All of us were hungry, but late daughter Adwoa was her usual hungry self.

She told me that she was hungry, and I assured her that her mom was cooking. Though her mom was laboring hard in the kitchen, for Adwoa, the food was not being prepared fast enough.

As we waited for the food to be ready, she kept asking me when it would be time for us to begin eating. I told her that it would be a little while because Mommy just started cooking.

A short while later, she asked: "Daddy, when is Mommy going to finish cooking?" "In a few minutes," I replied. One minute later, she again asked, "Daddy, when is the food coming?" "In just a little while," I replied wearingly.

Since she continued to annoy me, I told her to sit tight and not bother me any longer. After this caution, she kept quiet for a little while. When I thought, she was done bombarding me with questions, she came back and said, "Daddy, can Mommy make the food cook faster?"

Just like my late daughter, many times we pose the same type of questions to God, "Father, can you make time go faster? I'm so tired of waiting. I'm anxious for my prayer to be answered. Please make it arrive sooner." But we fail to realize that God's timing is different from ours. God had this message for the early Christians, and he gives the same to us today: "With the Lord, a day is like a thousand years, and a thousand years are like a day.

The Lord is not slow in keeping his promise, as some understand slowness. Instead, he is patient with you, not wanting anyone to perish, but everyone to come to repentance" (2 Peter 3:8-9). The lesson we can take from this is that, though waiting is painful, there are drawbacks to rushing actions. Therefore, whether you are an adult making a major life decision or a child requesting something from your parents, you need to exercise patience because it has so many inherent merits.

THE IRRITATION OF WAITING

Looking at the drawbacks of impatience, waiting should be highly recommended. However, we cannot deny the fact that waiting has its irritations. Particularly for people who seem stuck in life and have become rudderless: Like the homeless man in chapter one, or Lux, who wasted all the opportunities that came their way, and now seem to have no direction in life; or people who lost opportunities because they waited too long.

Such people may have little incentive to wait. They will be irritated with waiting. Even for people who have managed their time well, waiting is still irksome. Thus no one delights in waiting. Nevertheless, before you decide that you are tired of waiting, sit down and contemplate your actions. The irritation of waiting can push you to make rushed decisions that you could later regret. This irritation is the more reason why you should wait for the right moment to take a step into the world of the unknown.

WAITING FOR THE RIGHT MOMENT

Many people find themselves in a rat race of some sort. They get so fearful and worried that things are not going the way they want. All humans are guilty of this shortcoming. In our quest for instant progress, we never stop to consider the best-case scenarios. Sometimes we simply do not stop to ask God because we know that if we do, he will say no. Nevertheless, sometimes that is the answer we need.

Peggy and Catherine were two siblings who loved the Lord. Their love for the Lord was so infectious. Peggy, the eldest, went on to College after High School. Catherine, on the other hand, found a nice country boy to marry after High School. By the time Peggy finished college, her sister Catherine had already settled down to family life.

When Peggy finished college, she found a teaching position in the same city where they grew up together. Once Peggy gained some roots at the institution where she was teaching, she had the desire to marry and settle down to a happy family life. The years went by, and her search turned out with no husband. She would come and see me at the office, and the two of us would pray about her desire.

Unfortunately, days turned into months and months into years, but still, there was no suitor. Sometime later, Peggy started growing cold in her love for the Lord. She was no longer as frequent at church as she used to be. One day during those times, she came to church with a man whom she said was the person she wanted to marry. I told her how happy I was for her that now she had found somebody.

However, in our church at that time, we had a six-month-long premarital counseling before couples could perform the wedding at the church. Peggy thought the six-month waiting period was too long. That day she left my office with a long face. The next thing I heard, Peggy was married to that man and living with him. Not long after she got married, Peggy was diagnosed with HIV.

At that time, antiretroviral drugs that fought against HIV and AIDS were not discovered. Peggy was a fighter, but after some struggles, she succumbed to HIV AIDS and died. To this day, I believe Peggy decided to marry that stranger because of the peer pressure that was brought to bear on her by friends and relatives. She was seen as an odd one because she waited for so long for a partner.

It is always hard when you become the odd one out because you will not do what everybody is doing. But if you can stand the taunts and the threats, in the end, the Lord will make your righteous reward shine like the dawn, your vindication like the noonday sun. David advised, "Be still before the Lord and wait patiently for him; do not fret when people succeed in their ways when they carry out their wicked schemes" (Psalm 37:7).

Sometimes it might seem that your friends are leaving you behind because they are cutting corners and succeeding at it. Don't you worry; you are not your friends; you are a child of God, so you cannot act like some of your friends who do not seem to mind that what they are doing does not glorify God.

Waiting can be painful and agonizing. However, if you can gather the strength to wait, it will eventually be worthwhile. You can glean a glimpse of this if you pay particular attention to the mutation of the caterpillar into a butterfly. This beautiful creature, though made to fly has to go through four stages of metamorphosis to become a full-blown butterfly: it begins as an egg, then is hatched as a caterpillar, then as a cocoon before it can finally emerge as a beautiful butterfly.

The preacher said, "To everything, there is a season, a time for every purpose under heaven" (Ecclesiastes 3: 1). Often, we want to walk straight into a top management position. We want to be like some people who have achieved greatness in society, but we want to skip the journey to take us to the destination where we see those who are successful before us. When we behave like this, it means that we have forgotten that a caterpillar blooms into a butterfly over time.

It should be evident to us that there are risks to anything being born prematurely. For anything to be born, whether it is a vision or a calling, we who are to fulfill it must go on a journey. We must go through stages and seasons of preparation. We must wait for the right time for all the training to come to fruition.

There is a story of a young man who went into a corporation with the hopes of working in management. Conversely, when he reported for work on his first day, he was assigned to empty trash and do other menial jobs around the office. At first, he felt insulted and wanted to walk right out of the office. However, on impulse, he decided to stay and carry out those demeaning tasks. As he approached this job with all the diligence, he was noticed by his superiors. Before long, he was promoted from one position to another. Soon he was in upper management. All that would not have been possible had he walked away on the first day.

This said, however, the fact remains that waiting can be painful. However, whilst those who wait are eventually rewarded, those who are impatient are often disappointed.

WAITING IS A SHOW OF STRENGTH

If you can wait, it shows your depth of strength. It is weak-willed individuals who show impatience and are unable to wait. The writer of Hebrews says that without faith, it is impossible to please God. Anyone who has faith waits and hopes because he or she knows that God is faithful. So, as you wait, do not give up hope but believe that the God who has promised is faithful.

Hindsight is always twenty-twenty. We can always look back and point accusing fingers at those who have gone ahead of us. What we forget is that all humans err in the business of waiting for our turn. History is littered with examples of people who failed to wait with dire consequences.

Some leaders have rushed their countries into wars that were not necessary and were then unable to get out. Both the Russian Federation and the USA have gone to war with Afghanistan and got embroiled in a never-ending civil war.

In antiquity also, the people of Israel suffered from severe retribution for their inability to wait for their leader Moses to reappear from the mountain where he had gone to pray for forty days. In their impatience, they pressured Aaron to make them a god who would go before them. Because they could not wait for the Lord, all those who were impatient and sought another god perished in the wilderness.

Waiting is always rewarding. Joshua, Caleb, and the Israelis, who waited patiently for God's timing, eventually inherited the promised land, while people like Dathan and Abiram, who could not wait for the inheritance of God, were consumed in the wilderness.

The reward for people who have waited for the right timing is immense. When you wait for your dream instead of settling for a second choice, you realize your potential. This notion is exemplified by the 1939 film, "A Little Princess." This film, adapted from Frances Hodgson Burnett's book "A Little Princes," has young Sara Crewe, played by Shirley Temple, placed in the care of Amanda Minchin, the head of an exclusive seminary for girls, when her father, Captain Crewe, goes off to fight in the Boer War.

This is a reversal-of-fortune movie because whilst her father is at war, little Sara lives a privileged life and is quite happy in her surroundings.

However, when news filtered in that her father is listed as missing in action, her life goes from one of plenty to that of a poor housemaid. Mrs. Minchin, the friendly headmistress turned hostile host, grudgingly agrees to keep her on at the school.

Nevertheless, because her tuition payment was no longer forthcoming, she turned little Sara into a housemaid cleaning and scrubbing floors to earn a living. Though her former schoolmates sarcastically dubbed her the little princess she never caved in.

Sarah is resilient and does not give up in the face of hunger, depravation, and the hostile reception from the previously congenial headmistress. Convinced that her father was alive, she searched the area hospitals and eventually found him.

In the movie, Sara portrays a child with unshakable hope, patience, politeness, and kindness in the face of adversity. In her resolve to find her father, she meets Queen Victoria, who finds it hard to believe that a child under such duress could be so gracious. Who would believe that, being a pauper, she could meet the Queen of England?

All these are possible because the little girl held on to her hope that, eventually, things would turn out well. Her attitude showed someone who tried to make the best of a very bad situation, all the while holding on to her faith and never giving up hope.

Whilst this is just a movie, there is a virtue in exercising patience and hoping that God will bring into fruition his plan and purpose for our lives. In the time of waiting, you will be given a new lease on life which you might not have had before. This renewed vision and strength will reenergize you to greater heights.

HOLD ON TO UNDYING HOPE

We have seen how essential waiting is to human development. However, if you wait without hoping that things will get better, you are waiting in vain. Hoping implies that you are always prepared to hold unflinchingly to your belief despite the challenges that will come your way. You hold on because you trust and believe that your patience will be rewarded.

Thus, it may seem that people who can hold on when things have deteriorated are out of this world. No, they are people just like you. Nevertheless, they can hold on and stay hopeful, because they have certain core values that are unassailable by doubt and pessimism.

They can energize their lives in the face of challenges. They negotiate the rough and tumble roads and pay no heed to diversions. When they come to a *cul-de-sac*, they still find reason to keep on hoping. It is such a resolve that will impact your life. Like those who have succeeded before you, you have greatness in you; your destiny is carved in your moments of adversity more than in your times of bliss. In adversity, if you can wait and contemplate your fate, you can truly nurture your true self.

You were not created to be a minnow in society. It is an ascription in which you choose yourself when you fail to accept who you are and instead settle for the second best. Accordingly, you should hold steady to hope for a better future because in the face of trials and tribulations, if you persist, you will eventually realize your destiny.

Moreover, exercise your hope in faith because ardent faith will keep your hope alive. This perseverance in hope will help you garner the strength to be an overcomer. If you easily give up hope; if you put little value on waiting, you have very little chance of consolidating your life's gains.

Hence, if you have to choose between hoping and giving up, hold on to undying hope because it is your salvation. The biblical character Job, in his affliction, never gave up hope. As he waited with his body wasting away, he held on to the hope that things were going to get only better.

He found similarities between a shoot sprouting and bearing fruit and humans reimagining their destinies. If a stump can bud again, a human can do even better no matter how low they have sunk, he reasoned. Like the tree, you too can sprout and prosper if you can hold on to undying hope.

CHAPTER EIGHT

TACTFULNESS HAS POSITIVE BENEFITS

"Tact is the ability to step on a man's toes without messing up the shine on his shoes."
Harry S. Truman

TAKING THE TACTFUL APPROACH

When Lisa pulled into the parking lot at her workplace, she was already an hour late. Therefore, as soon as she parked, she rushed to her office. The mood as she entered was drab. Lisa worked in a call center that catered to a large clientele of banks, credit card, and cable companies. The subdued atmosphere was due to a serial caller unsatisfied with their services barging in to raise everybody's anxiety level.

Ordinarily, customers are not allowed into the center. Nevertheless, occasionally a troubled customer manages to find their location and comes in to cause trouble. This was one such morning. This man had managed to elude security and come in to vent his frustration to the customer service personnel. His anger and antagonism had dampened the spirits of the entire office staff.

Though this was not an uncommon occurrence, today's visitor was unusually loud and abusive. Due to his offensive language, every one of them was down. Lisa was usually the person who dealt with such difficult people, so her delay was particularly felt by her co-workers. Shortly after settling down, she ushered the man into her small cubicle space, which she called her office.

After an hour of talking to him, the visitor emerged from Lisa's office, beaming with smiles. Lisa did not do anything special. However, the calmness of her voice and her tactfulness got this angry customer to calm down. At the end of the conversation, Lisa did not only get him to understand things but also sold him more service.

What the customer was looking for was somebody who would listen to him. This, he found in Lisa, who not only showed a calm presence but also dealt with him discreetly. This tactful approach that Lisa took is what is needed in relationships in our fast-paced and changing world.

In today's world, people appear to have less time at their disposal than they did in previous generations. In more ways than one, we are unwilling to stop and listen to the next person. This has surely made communication almost impossible. This development calls for tactfulness in all our dealings with others. If you want to make it in our current fast-paced world, you ought to be tactful and smart like Lisa.

Tact, which is the ability to be right on cue, is needed more now than ever before because of our limited attention span. There are two ways of expressing tact. When one is guarded in speech and manner, he is regarded as tactful. Conversely, anyone whose manners are awkward, or who uses language without regard to the feelings of others is being tactless.

The preferable behavior that brings people together is that of tactfulness. If you are tactful, you have a knack for saying and doing the right thing at the right time. Also, you are sensitive to the needs and circumstances of others, always using language appropriately and seeking to bring harmony to explosive situations.

Moreover, you are never rude or careless in your dealings with others. In short, being tactful is the ability to say the right thing at the right time. It is, therefore, a gift displayed in one's speech and manners because he understands what the situation calls for.

Tactful people are very conservative with words; they do not freely volunteer criticisms, and they do their best to treat others with sensitivity and thoughtfulness. If they must criticize, they thread very cautiously. Their careful approach ensures that they achieve much with little or no acrimony. Interestingly, tact does not only involve the things that you say but also involves those things left unsaid.

WHEN TO APPLY TACT

Tactfulness can be shown in many situations, particularly when a friend or an acquaintance falls into uncomfortable circumstances. When there is news of a mishap such as death, sickness, or accident resulting in the loss of property and life, the victim requires the most help or comfort. At such times the tactful person will promptly be at the side of the victim and offer any immediate assistance that will be needed. These times when one is sick or loses a loved one are the times that need to be handled with the greatest care.

When an acquaintance is in trouble, it is easy to be talkative and say something insensitive. Please refrain from saying, 'I know how you feel' because you don't. A reaction that is opposite to the behavior of the tactful in times when our acquaintances need our support is that which the tactless display. Normally, when they hear a friend or an acquaintance is in trouble, they will stay away. Those people who stay away do not only lose face with the friend who was in trouble but also the people associated with this friend who knew of their previous relationship.

For this person who stayed away, the next time they see their friend, it presents an awkward moment. Their discomfort comes from the fact that they would have to find a way to apologize for their insensitivity. Such a person loses credibility not only with the friend but others who may be familiar with what transpired.

Another time when tact is needed is in a conflict situation. We are familiar with Lisa's approach that helped her to diffuse a volatile situation. Lisa tactfully admitted her company's wrongdoings and promptly apologized. It is precisely what any tactful person will do in such situations. On the other hand, Lisa's colleagues, being tactless, were dragging the issue and thus were turning anthills into mountains.

Conversely, Lisa continued to show tact throughout the conversation. She thanked the visitor for being so understanding and considerate. This approach disarmed the troublemaker and caused him to consider his unreasonableness towards Lisa's company. Besides his embarrassment, he felt indebted to Lisa for his recalcitrance and compensated for that by returning the favor shown to him by Lisa. His response was to order more service.

Moreover, whereas previously he had been rude to the others, in Lisa's case, he was shamed for his actions and profusely apologized to her for his earlier uncivil behavior. It is expedient to note that tact does not come in handy only in one-on-one situations like the one that transpired between Lisa and the customer. Even in groups, it plays such dynamics that the tactful person can use her skill to put herself in the limelight.

This application of tact was exemplified in its usage during the beginning of the Roman Republic. This was a period that was marked by internal squabbles between the patricians, who were the aristocrats, and the plebeians or working-class citizens.

Those confrontations involved exchanges that portrayed the skillful use of language. The situation brought out the best use of language that not only employed flowery and sophistication,[20] as George Kennedy alludes to but also demonstrated wisdom and tact.

It is noteworthy that tact does not only involve what we say. At certain times not saying anything at all is better than a thousand words. Those situations include times when you disagree with another person, during heated arguments, or even during bereavement. In such situations, if you do not have a word that will calm the circumstances or, in the case of the bereaved, assurance, then refrain from speaking. Situations where people are angry call for great tact. When you speak whilst you are angry, you give the other party ammunition they can use against you in the future.

THE SCOPE OF TACTFULNESS

Tactfulness, when shown in speeches, displays verbal acumen that can be used to diffuse any conflict. A classic example of how tact was employed in conflict situations was the masterful speech of Mark Anthony when addressing the assailants of Julius Caesar.

Generally, people who display verbal distinction are not only accepted by the general populace but are also able to ingratiate themselves with the power brokers in society. Any of us can attain this distinction through study,

---

20. Kennedy, Rhetoric in the Roman, 4.

and by seeking to use language imaginatively. It is in such situations that we can conveniently describe anybody as tactful.

When that person can turn his thoughts into words without offending another person. Because she does not speak unnecessarily, she chooses her words with the utmost caution. It is a skill that can help one enrich her relationships. Tactfulness is useful in several ways. It helps us to make and keep friends. It also helps us to prolong our lives because we do not go around making enemies because of certain actions or inaction of ours.

Tactfulness mainly involves the expert handling of three things that are important in any speech: the formation of one's thoughts, the communication of those thoughts, and the effecting of understanding. The tactful person in his or her dealings causes fewer bruises and opens fewer wounds. Such a person is not only respected but revered. Furthermore, he or she is not simply labeled tactfully but perceptively. Remember this, whenever a speech leads to rancor and discord, triumph is thrown through the window.

In this vein, whenever you are interacting with others, do not be hasty to speak your mind. Because words, once spoken, can never be retracted. And words that are spoken in haste may have unintended consequences. If you are unguarded and make a disparaging remark about another person, it may haunt you all your life. Words are like arrows; they can inflict mortal wounds. They are also like a balm; they can heal and bolster the confidence of another person. Therefore, if you must speak, your words should foster confidence and not foment skepticism; they must build, not pull down.

Tactfulness also implies being able to speak properly and intelligibly. It is one of the many ways for people to get ahead in life. To ascertain this, it would be good to take a closer look at some ancient cultures, such as the Greco-Romans. They had three main goals for any speech "to instruct, to move, and to delight."[21] This notion of the ancient Greeks has become the bedrock of the modern public speaking movement. It is a guideline for politicians, teachers, and preachers.

The person who is eloquent in speech and can apply wisdom in her interaction with others is the one who can move people in her speech. El-

---

21. Quintilian II: The Orator's Education Books 3-5 Edited and Translated by Donald A. Russell. Cambridge, Massachusetts and London England: Harvard University Press, 2001, 39).

oquence should, therefore, work in tandem with tact to make any speech highly effective.

THE ROLE OF TACT IN COMMUNICATION

Tactfulness plays a positive role in any communication, whether at the individual level or in groups. To understand the role effective and tactful communication plays, it will be good to examine what three eminent speech practitioners have said about the topic.

One of the prominent practitioners of eloquence in the ancient world was Aristotle. He saw eloquence as one's ability to masterfully express his views about any subject and make sense to his audience. To Aristotle, the speaker must observe the available means of persuasion. In other words, Aristotle wants the speaker to study the people and the circumstances to guide him to choose his words. Any speaker who is successful in doing this will always be on cue and would therefore be understood.

George Kennedy, a modern writer of speech and Rhetoric, on the other hand, sees eloquence as imparting both mental and emotional energy to a speech. This energy, he claims, works to the advantage of the speaker because it helps him drive home his point. The force of his definition is in its focus on communication. The impartation of mental and emotional energy in the communication process should be a major preoccupation of any speech. It should reinforce the communication process by using different rhetorical tools such as repetition, figure of speech, and tropes, among others.

Invariably, a good speech is not to the advantage of the speaker only, as Kennedy claims, but to the mutual advantage of both speaker and hearer.

The third definition comes from the Bulgarian French historian and philosopher Tzvetan Todorov. He claims that eloquence ensures effective communication and leaves the other party to react positively to situations. In a similar vein, Todorov's definition aims at the effective use of the tools of speechmaking to give force to the communication process. His view that the subject deals with the function of speech and not the structure could be contestable, though.

A good speech depends on how it is structured as well as what it accomplishes. Therefore, in any speechmaking, both the function and structure should be deemed equally important. No doubt, Aristotle, Kennedy, and Todorov are clear about the role that effective communication can have in the life of any individual. They show that effective speeches empower the communication process providing the medium for people to communicate their ideas forcefully.

Thus, effective speechmaking is one in which communication is carried on to the point of influencing both the transmission and reception of information so that the two become mutually and inclusively beneficial. When speeches are effective, they are tactfully crafted so that they not only curry the favor of their audience, but the audience is also made favorably disposed towards the speaker.

In this vein, if you are an aspiring public speaker, your goal for a speech and the response to the speech should be agreeable. In other words, at the end of your speech, both you and your listeners should have mutual satisfaction. To be able to make an impact on others, therefore, your speech should be seasoned with salt, so to speak.

The able politician, actor, teacher, or preacher is the one who has become proficient at her subject and is masterfully able to convey it across a cross-section of people and be understood by all parties. This understanding can be fostered through the application of skill and tact in any speech. As a person who is involved in any speaking role, avoid any ambiguities and language that can be misconstrued by any member of the audience.

It should be noted that the application of tact is not limited to only public figures. The simple reason is that speech is the best form of communication between parties. So, whenever one interacts with another, it involves speech. In this area, it is always good for people to be mindful of their words so as not to put others off.

Remarkably, tactfulness does not have anything to do with flattery. Though the word of God counsels the believer to season his or her speech with salt, it also urges them to always show graciousness. Thus, God's word does not in any way allude to flattery.[22]

THE BENEFITS OF BEING TACTFUL

Certainly, if you want to determine an authentic and cultured person, you need not look beyond the tactful person. Those people do not hide behind any false identity. They are confident and self-assured. They possess the skills that they not only use to advance the course of society but also to uplift their image in the social order.

Tactful people open their mouths with wisdom and make themselves available as kind-hearted mentors, teaching others the way to prosperity and tranquility. If one has mastered the intricacies of applying tact in his speech, he can easily defend himself against any accusations of wrongdoing on any and every occasion.

Individuals can singularly apply tact to their benefit. They can also apply it to benefit groups or even nations. People who employ tact in all aspects of life are not simply viewed as astute and wise but are also revered. Because their actions do not simply put them in good stead, but also help foster unity and peace.

Very often, the actions of the tactful build bridges between people of opposing views as well as those of differing political persuasions. Typical of tactful people were the *stratēgos*[23] of Ancient Greece. They derived their name through their thought-provoking and inspiring speeches that united and motivated their people to present a united front during wartime.

When people are tactful, it is not only the individual who benefits, sometimes, nations are the beneficiaries. We can see this in many Bible stories where tact is employed both positively and negatively for the course of a nation. Here, we shall take a closer look at two such stories.

The first story is about an unnamed woman in the town of Abel. This woman was referred to as the wise woman of Abel because of her skillful

---

22. Cf. Colossians 4:6 HYPERLINK "https://www.biblegateway.com/passage/?search=Colossians+4%3A6&version=ESV"

23. Russell, D. A. Greek Declamation [Cambridge: Cambridge University Press, 1982], 22.

use of language. David, the king of Israel, was facing a rebellion from his son Absalom.

Fortunately, Absalom was killed in battle with King David's men. When the war was over, the people of Israel contemplated bringing the king back to Jerusalem in a triumphant procession. However, Israel was upstaged by the tribe of Judah who went ahead to bring the king back to his palace.

The actions of the Judeans displeased the rest of Israel, and they made their displeasure known to them. In the ensuing argument, a man named Sheba led a revolt. Joab, David's army commander, though deposed by the king in his role of killing his son Absalom, managed to take charge again of the army and pursued Sheba and his forces.

Meanwhile, Sheba and his forces had taken refuge in a town called Abel. As the town came under siege from Joab's forces, this wise woman of Abel managed to convince Joab to stay his hand. Using her skill at language, she got the people to murder Sheba and thereby avert imminent destruction.

The second story is about Rehoboam, the son of Solomon, king of Israel. Solomon came to the throne with high hopes after he had shown much devotion to God. Unfortunately, during his reign, he subjected the people to an austere life to support his excesses. So, when Solomon died, the people came to his son and successor to plead with him to lighten their load.

Rehoboam consulted both the elders and his friends, who gave him various advice. Later he spurned the advice of the elders and took that of his contemporaries. He was very tactless and careless. He responded to the people: "My little finger is thicker than my father's waist. My father laid on you a heavy yoke; I will make it even heavier. My father scourged you with whips; I will scourge you with scorpions'" (1 Kings 12:10-11).

In these two situations, we see the different shades of the use of tact. Whilst one used tact to positively convey a thoughtful reaction to defuse a volatile situation, the other rushed his answers tactlessly to inflame an explosive situation. Proverbs 15:28 says: "The heart of the righteous ponders how to answer, but the mouth of the wicked pours out evil things."

This underscores the need for people confronted with dicey situations to thoughtfully consider their words before they seek to provide any answers. Due to the tactful use of words, the woman's actions did not only save a town but ensured a united kingdom. Rehoboam, on the other hand, was tactless with words and divided a kingdom.

The foregone brings to the fore that those who are tactful not only receive admiration but also assist others in striving for common goals. However, the same cannot be said for the tactless because they only bring chaos and division.

THE APPROPRIATE USE OF TACT

There are appropriate and inappropriate uses of tactfulness. As an individual, if you appropriately apply tact, you stand to benefit greatly. To use tact appropriately, you will need to eschew bluntness in all situations. One such situation is when a friend or an acquaintance asks you to express an honest opinion about them. Even such occasions demand the utmost caution because if you are unguarded in your words, you can greatly damage them.

If the situation requires that you tell them the truth they are looking for, do it in such a way that at the end of proceedings, you do not lose them through the employment of some unguarded words. At this time that you are being asked for your honest opinion you may feel that it is an opportunity to blur out what you think of that person.

However, when such opportunities are offered, you should show love and tact by withholding whatever information may be damaging to the confidence of the person who asked for your opinion. If you must be truthful with such inquiries, then do your best to tailor whatever criticisms you have to the barest minimum so that the person may not feel bruised in the end.

In this dilemma of helping your friend, consider Sir Isaac Newton's words: "Tact is the art of making a point without making an enemy." Therefore, when the situation calls for it, be kind with your assessment and do not lose your friend because you misspoke.

Another appropriate use of tact, is to treat all people fairly without regard to race or ethnicity, wealth, or poverty. If you treat people differently because they look different from you or because of their societal standing, you surely debase yourself in their eyes.

Additionally, using tact appropriately can be seen in the way you treat your subordinates. In such dealings, you should guard against being seen as arrogant and uncaring. Since you are in a position of authority, sometimes your subordinates may not be frank with you because they may want to curry your favor. Therefore, they might sometimes be tempted to lie to you so as not to offend you. So, don't be gullible. Critically examine whatever advice they give you so that you will not be driven into an undesirable situation.

Moreover, in dealing with other people, you might unknowingly step on their feet. When that happens, you should be quick to apologize so that sanity will be restored. What would be inappropriate would be to act as a person who builds a fence around themselves when they know they are clearly in the wrong. As a further suitable action, insulate yourself against any future attacks others might mount against you by being quick to recognize your mistakes and making amends where possible.

An additional appropriate use of tact is to guard against any tendency to be opinionated or self-conceited. If you have been arrogant and self-conceited at any point in your life, you will clearly understand what tact can do for you. People who are big-headed, disrespectful, and egotistical characters easily lose their standing in society. In most cases, people seldom voluntarily offer their help to people like that. Even when they can get others to aid them, they do it grudgingly.

Conversely, those who are tactful and considerate willingly get others to offer them their help. Such people, as a validation of what they stand for, get others to willingly help without requesting them. As Angelica Hopes shows, "Arrogance, disrespect, and demand have higher price, [but] kindness, respect, and tact give a better prize."[24]

Know that it is never too late to use tact appropriately. The reason is that the fact that you may have let down your guard at one time or another does not mean you cannot change. As humans, we always make mistakes. Show me the person who does not make mistakes, and I will show you a perfect person. Hence, do not let your past mistakes haunt you. Instead, your desire should

---

24. An Angelica Hopes quotes<goodreads.com/author/show/4491145. Angelica Hopes accessed January 31, 2015

be to use tact appropriately in all your interactions. Therefore, begin today to strive in that direction and see how things will turn out for you in no time.

Your success will not only ensure a prolonged life but will also give you a life of harmony and bliss. Besides, since you know what to say and when to say it, you are very unlikely to get into trouble with anyone who may want to plan evil for you. When all is said, knowing when to apply tact will boost your confidence and make your way forward smoother. If you check out all the right boxes in both your speech and manner, it will elevate your standing in society and make you an affable person to live with.

CHAPTER NINE

THERE IS A MIRACLE IN GIVING

"There is no exercise better for the heart than reaching down and lifting people."
John Holmes

THE HUMAN SPIRIT OF SHOWING GENEROSITY

Maude, married for 39 years to her high school sweetheart, could not have children, so they entered the adoption market. They were fortunate to adopt a couple of orphaned children, shortly before her husband passed away. Though the death of her husband affected her financially, Maude was determined to give the children a new home. Now with her husband gone, she devoted her time to caring for her children.

Maude's giving bucked the trend because she not only gave money, but she also gave love and affection to children who were otherwise devoid of it. Again, she showed that one need not necessarily be rich to give. If the willingness is there, anybody can be generous. Thus, through her giving Maude showed the poor can equally give to others. Not only did she show us who a generous person can be, but she also showed that giving to others should not all be about money but also love and affection.

Accordingly, in her humble example, Maude displayed the human spirit to show generosity. Her action further depicted that giving does not only involve the exchange of money or material things but also involves an individual's selflessness about others. Moreover, her action showed that generosity, instead of being simply an act of giving financial or material assistance, becomes more than that of showing love towards another person.

Many rich people are generous, but sometimes people who are not so rich are relatively more generous. Though one rich person may give more than thousands of what a poorer person can, if measured against their contribution is smaller than the latter's. Rich people give out of the abundance of their wealth, while the poor give more than their net worth.

In this direction, whenever you are tempted to hold on when you know you can give more, or do more for another person, please do not hesitate to do so. The more you open to other people, the more you will be doing the will of Jesus, who emphasized that it is more rewarding to give than to receive. People with a generous spirit do not only have a volunteering spirit or the giving of financial incentives. Rather they embrace a lot of other forms of giving. All the different forms of generosity contribute to the make-up of the generous person.

Those who are generous are always looking for opportunities and avenues where they can be of help to others and society. It is an act of making oneself in one's relationships available to other people so that their needs can be met. Generosity can be a form of virtual circle: what goes around comes around. The teacher urges the believer to cast his bread upon the waters with the hope of getting it back at a future date. Wealth does not necessarily bring happiness and fulfillment. However, the wealthy person who gives out her wealth to help others gains untold happiness and is eventually fulfilled.

THE HEART OF GENEROSITY

At the heart of giving is the desire to help those disadvantaged in life. That was what Maude showed, supporting her adopted children with her meager income. Though some people give with strings attached, a vast majority of people who give are motivated by a desire to help their fellow humans. They do so out of a grateful heart. Often, their prime motivation is to help those less privileged find their feet so that they can also contribute to the well-being of society.

Many people have a generous spirit, and they desire to make the world a better place for everybody. Therefore, they give their time, service, and money to help others so that life might be bearable for as many people as possible. Also core to generosity is the desire of some people to choose austerity to be of help to others. Their examples offer a refreshing anecdote to the sordid story of human fallibility.

Take the story of Percy Ross, the son of a junk dealer in Minnesota who lived a rather tough life growing up. In his adult life, however, he became very rich when he bought and saved a plastic bag company from going bankrupt. Nevertheless, Ross lost as much money as he made by giving it out to people he saw as needy. At one Christmas party, he gave out more than a thousand bikes to children. Besides this, at another time, he gave out nearly $20,000 to onlookers at a local parade.

On top of all these, he felt he needed to do more so he started a newspaper column which he titled, "Thanks a Million," with the sole aim of reaching out to a wider spectrum of people he could help. The column—which ran in 800 newspapers for 16 years—was a massive success and saw thousands of people write and ask Ross for money. Oftentimes, he gleefully handed money and checks in person to those he felt needed help, but he did not hesitate to turn down requests from people whom he thought had the means to get the money for themselves. When he died in 2001, he had nothing to his name, having given out over $30 million. In his last column before his death, he expressed his happiness at being able to share his fortune with those who needed it.

At the heart of showing kindness should be the desire to help others irrespective of whether they are family or friends, whether or not they look like you, or share the same creed or religion. Ideally, the act of kindness begins with one's immediate environment and then extends beyond family or friends, tribe or nation.

In your desire to adhere to the best principles for giving, you should be guided by what God did on behalf of people. His love for the world led him to give his only Son so that the person who believes escapes the crutches of death and is instead rewarded with eternal life. God did not take that initiative because he needed or desired something from us. Rather, he did that out of his abounding love. That should be at the heart of your giving.

You limit the power of your giving if you harbor ulterior motives or attach strings to them.

In giving, however, we should be guided by the simple fact that there is a variance in human abilities and wealth. For that reason, the expedient thing to do is for those lucky to be endowed with wealth and substance to offer help to those who are less fortunate.

DIFFERENT WAYS OF SHOWING GENEROSITY

There are different ways to show generosity. It can be in cash or kind; to an individual or a group. We can also show generosity when we give to churches and organizations or even to a country. When we pay tithes and offerings to a church, we help to support the ministries of that church. Similarly, when we pay our taxes to a country, we are helping to support that country's development and services.

In every country, there are the rich and the poor. One way that nations correct the imbalance is to institute progressive tax systems where people pay taxes proportionate to their income. When the rich people generously pay their taxes, it goes to support the development of the infrastructure of the country such as roads, health, and sports facilities. These facilities go to help everybody, including the disadvantaged who otherwise could not have financed efficient healthcare systems or built roads to facilitate movement.

Another way of showing generosity is to give your support to a person giving a speech. If you have spoken in public before, you will know the value of moral support. Though I have preached for over twenty years, anytime I stand before a group of people to preach, I am full of fear and trepidation. I may not be alone in this area. Most people experience this fear.

However, if when you are preaching you get others cheering you on, it buoys you on to preach the word boldly. This inadequacy is not peculiar to preachers alone; rather, any public speaker suffers from these blues.

Therefore, the next time you see somebody giving a public presentation, give them all the encouragement you can. Avoid making faces, fidgeting, or checking the clock to see how much time he or she is wasting. Rather make it a habit to give moral support whenever you possibly can. Other ways of showing generosity include sharing your knowledge and experience with others.

Without a doubt, your confidence and happiness level will increase when you see how the information you share with others has given their lives a new meaning. As a person with a kind heart, look out for needy and deserving people around you and help them out.

Giving should not all be about money. Most of us are not able to give because we deceptively think that all there is to give to others is money. Have you forgotten the encounter between Peter and John with the panhandler at the Golden Gate? These men had something marvelous to offer him, but all he wanted was a few coins with which he could buy some food or clothing. Peter and John, however, had something greater in mind. They offered him the means to be able to get up and make money for himself. In the name of Jesus, they healed him of his crippling sickness.

That is what people with five-star personalities do. They give other people a chance. Today you can give somebody hope by saying some kind words to them. You can energize somebody by simply patting them on the back. Make up your mind not to take the limelight all the time. Rather strive to motivate others to develop their talents and abilities. Brighten people's days by smiling at them. A smile can have magical powers. It can encourage people to brighten up and motivate them to be the best they can be.

THE BENEFITS OF ACTS OF KINDNESS

Acts of kindness have the power to transform both the giver and the receiver in profound ways. It meets the needs of the beneficiary while at the same time giving the donor the satisfaction of knowing that his or her compassion has positively affected a life.

There is an uplifting aspect in giving. When you give, it does not only change the state of the receiver, but it also affects the giver in ways that can be refreshing. It can change a coldhearted person into a loving and caring one more open to the needs of others. They, therefore, have a transformative power on the giver, making him or her a person who looks out for the good of the society in which they live. It is, therefore, a formidable heritage that can turn the most callous person into a warmhearted one.

When you discover the spirit of giving, you will also discover the miracle associated with it. It makes you experience the real joy of seeing others' lives coming together or getting the energy to go about their daily business. You will thus experience amazing growth in your life. This might have appropriately spelled out the feeling of the young boy who gave his five loaves of bread and two fishes to Jesus to multiply in the Judean countryside, to feed a multitude.

This young boy could have kept his food for himself knowing they were in an isolated place. However, because he generously provided them, he would have had great satisfaction in having a hand in that miraculous event. Like this boy, generosity is instilled in some people so that they are always willing to do acts that will put smiles back on the faces of the poor and needy.

To gain a proper understanding of how a person's life is impacted by kindness, let us look at the subject of salinity. This subject deals with the quantity of salt that is dissolved in a body of water. The sea has a high salinity of 35 parts per thousand (ppt)[25] percentage compared to that of any river which on average is only about 0.5 ppt. The sea's high salinity is attributed to the fact that it only receives water from other sources while giving nothing in return. Hence, it accumulates high concentrations of salt.

Conversely, a river always empties its waters into another river or the sea. For this reason, rivers offer more value to humans as compared to the sea. Rivers offer sources of drinking water for humans and their animals, whilst the sea is useless for drinking. The uses of the sea to humanity are more limited, such as serving as a channel for travel and maintaining the atmospheric circulation of rain-bearing weather systems.

What we can learn from this is that anybody who is always receiving and not giving anything in return can become bloated and, with time, implode from within. Furthermore, you should be aware that your failure to give will hinder you from receiving anything in the long term.

---

25. Parts per thousand or ppt, is the standard measure for salinity concentrations.

The foregoing does not mean that those who benefit from the goodwill of the benevolent person are any less than that. When they receive from others, it also has a transformative power over them as beneficiaries. It make them appreciative of the goodwill that others show. It also can change their perspective regarding the affluent in society. Likewise, the help they receive when they are in need help lift them and give them the motivation to rediscover their potential.

Furthermore, they gain a sense of indebtedness to society. In that case, once they get out of their dire situations, they will no longer think only about their own needs but will also consider the needs of others. Recipients also feel gratitude towards the benefactors and acquire the sense to remain loyal to them forever.

Generosity, though, has several advantages and disadvantages both for the giver and the receiver; if it is not given or received with good intentions, it renders the act useless. As a giver, if you give with an unselfish attitude, you gain unsuspecting returns. With the same token, the receiver who receives with malice accrues untold hardships.

The Bible says: "One person gives freely, yet gains even more; another withholds unduly, but comes to poverty. A generous person will prosper; whoever refreshes others will be refreshed" (Proverbs 11:24-25). Nevertheless, let the quest for reward not be your reason for giving.

Similarly, if you are receiving help from others, make up your mind to also learn to give, because it is only by giving to others that you will also get out of your difficulty. Therefore, no matter what station you find yourself in life, cultivate a generous spirit by looking out for people who are in a less fortunate situation.

THE OBSTACLES TO GENEROUS GIVING

Looking at the benefits of giving, it should be safe to say that everybody should embrace it. This should be particularly true of those who could easily spare part of their wealth, time, or talent. The reason is that the poor amongst us are not all going away. Neither are all people going to have the same confidence level or even be in the same state of mind.

Human ability, as is our willingness to help others, is comparable to the structure of the fingers. These fingers have varying lengths and sizes relative to their functions. Similarly, the way we show generosity may be at different levels. For this reason, some people fail to give because they think their giving is insignificant.

One obstacle to generous giving is a lack of the spirit of generosity. It is not everybody who has a willingness to support others. Sometimes, we mistakenly think poor people are lazy and are probably on drugs, so we refuse to help even when we can. At other times, we believe that, if we show generosity, others might take advantage of our kindness. There are times we want to give, but we only limit our giving to our circle of friends and family. This type of giving makes you insular and blinded to the needs of people outside your immediate circle of friends and families.

Some others are not able to give because they would rather receive instead of giving away. Such people believe that they lose their life earnings by helping others and not saving what they have for their future needs. However, if you can overcome the desire to hold on to what you have and support others in their times of need, your life will be enriched in ways you never thought possible. Moreover, it is more fulfilling to give when you know you have satisfied somebody else's needs.

CHAPTER TEN

INVIGORATE YOUR LIFE THROUGH FAITH

*"Faith is taking the first step even when you
don't see the whole staircase."*
Martin Luther King, Jr.

FAITH—AN ESSENTIAL INGREDIENT FOR LIFE

Jim, his sister Abby, and his parents lived in a country house near Longmont, Colorado. Their house was surrounded by shrubs and a variety of fruit trees, including apples, apricots, plums, and avocados. Jim would sometimes climb onto one of the fruit trees to pick some fruit because the fruit picker was too heavy for either of them to use.

Jim's parents had seen him getting fruit from the trees on several occasions and had warned him against climbing trees. Though he had obeyed his parents' instructions, there were times he had a strong urge to collect fruit.

One afternoon, the two children sneaked out of the house to the farm to get some apples. In the process of getting the apples, Jim slipped from the trunk of the tree. It was only a branch he held on to that saved him from death or serious injury. Abby ran to the house to tell her parents about the accident, and they came running.

When their parents got to the farm, Jim was dangling on a branch that was about to snap. His father told him to let go of the branch to which he promptly obeyed, trusting his father to catch him. That is exactly what all humans do daily. Every human action is orchestrated by faith. We walk because we have faith that we will not sink into the earth's crust; we sit because we have faith that we will not fall. Moreover, we have faith that when we step out of our houses, we will return.

So, faith plays a vital role throughout our lifetime, propelling us to achieve the seemingly impossible. Nevertheless, if faith can play a meaningful role in your life, it would have to exceed that which you need to negotiate the daily hurdles. Your faith should be pregnant with such force that it can gather enough power to propel you to greater heights, beyond what you require for the simple acts of daily living. It should empower you to accept that all things are possible and available to you.

In other words, the faith you need is the faith that can move you from one station in life to another. It can do this by instilling in you a never-give-up spirit. To make it in life, you need to build this type of faith that will make you a winner. As you do this, there are two things you should recognize. The first is that progress is not achieved overnight, nor will putting limitations on your abilities help you. If you put limitations on your abilities or if you are impatient, you will be working your way to mediocrity.

Many people have been condemned to the bottom rungs of life because their faith is not able to carry them through tough times. Instead, when the going gets tough, they fold up and throw in the towel.

Conversely, those who have faith fight on knowing those circumstances are ephemeral. It will interest you to know that faith is not something you can quantify because it is of an immeasurable quantity. Therefore, there is no available means to measure how much faith you have. However, as you put your faith into action, your belief makes things possible. It translates the abstract into concrete, the intangible into tangible, and the elusive into the attainable. Therefore, recognize that you need to exercise your faith to make it grow.

WHY FAITH IS IMPORTANT

Faith is very important in our life. It is behind any achievement, any milestone that we make in life. It is important for your personal development and any enterprise you undertake in life. The difference between achievers and quitters is that while the former use their faith to achieve great things, the latter appeal to fear to destroy any chance of progress in their lives. The person who has faith sees challenges to future projects, whilst the one weak in faith sees obstacles. The perspective of these two people determine the progress that they make or do not make.

Thus, faith is essential for any achievement you can make in life. No matter which stage you are at with your faith, you can always build the faith that moves mountains by learning to speak and act positively. Never think anything is out of your reach. For if you only believe and not doubt, you can get your faith to work great things for you.

As humans, we cannot have the faith which God has. However, just exercising a fraction of our faith in God would get things going for us. You can speak to your mountain to move, and it will move. The dynamics involved in faith is that rewards are proportional to the amount of faith exercised.

Faith becomes important only when, in your time of need, it can save you. This only becomes possible when you take a leap of faith. You see, every human being has a reservoir of faith. This needs to be harnessed so that we can scale the numerous hurdles we encounter daily. Jesus told his disciples that even a little faith can lead to big achievements. For example, almost all birds can fly, but none can fly like the eagle. It can soar high on its wings because, as a predator bird, it thinks it is the master of all it surveys. Like the eagle, you, too, can soar to greater heights if you put your faith to work.

To benefit from the application of faith, don't look at your circumstances. Rather have an eye of faith to see beyond your present circumstances. Plato said, "We are twice armed if we fight with faith."[26] If you have faith, you will keep going even when others give up because faith sees what simple-minded people do not see. Notwithstanding the importance of faith, sometimes, because of past experiences, we fail to apply it when we are in trouble. Sometimes, you simply need to adapt the way you apply your faith. Go at it slowly, until you are sure that you have optimized the reach of your faith.

---

26. Plato Quote< http://www.brainyquote.com/photos/p/plato159576.jpg accessed October 22, 2015

OPTIMIZE YOUR FAITH

Because faith is essential not just for your daily survival but also for your prosperity, you ought to seek to optimize it. Optimizing your faith begins with your thought pattern. You are what you think about at any moment in your life. If you think defeat, that is what you will get. Similarly, if you think of abundance, it will come your way.

The way to optimize your faith is to turn your ideas into tangible items. All the objects you see around you came about because some other people turned their thoughts into things. Therefore, optimize your faith by turning your dreams from intangibles to concrete objects you can touch and feel. Move your impossibilities to possibilities, and your fantasies to reality. With an enhanced faith, things you thought were impossible always become possible.

To optimize your faith, you should put more trust in people, institutions, God, and, more importantly, in your abilities. When you boost your self-belief, you become dynamic in everything you do.

One way you can optimize your faith is to not walk away when matters get tough. When things become seemingly uncontrollable, your ability to stand firm and pursue positive ideals will greatly enhance your image in the eyes of both your detractors and admirers. Sometimes, you can lose faith in your abilities because of certain mistakes. However, these errors should not slow you down. Continue to be optimistic about yourself and other humans that we are all capable of giving out our very best.

At the same time, we are capable of evil. Therefore, if the unexpected happens to you, know that in all these, something good will come out of your situation. Remember, the uncertainties of life should neither keep you down nor slow the fulfillment of your life's goals. Optimize your faith to act as a catalyst for your personal growth, glue your marriage together, and facilitate and bring harmony to all your relationships.

THE FAITH TO BLOSSOM

When you optimize your faith, you can prevail over any obstacle and blossom. It will move you from a person who is always afraid to start anything new to one who is bold and adventurous. You will gain a better understanding of how a lack of faith can make you fail at even the easiest undertaking. As a demonstration of how faith or the lack thereof could affect a people, let us take examples from Israel's playbook. God had promised the land lying east of the Jordan River to them.

After their liberation from Egyptian bondage, they traveled for several days through the desert. Finally, on the verge of the Promised Land, Moses, their leader, sent twelve men, one from each tribe, to spy on the land before they invaded. These men roamed the length and breadth of the land and came back with a report covering the layout, the vegetation as well as the people who lived there. It was mainly objective without embellishment.

Nevertheless, at the tail end of their report, they preyed on the peoples' fears by telling them they were unable to go and conquer the people who lived there. They contended that the people of the land were giants. They compared themselves to those people and found themselves wanting. Instead of relying on God, they relied on their abilities. They brought chaos and unrest into the community because the people rebelled against Moses and selected leaders to lead them back to Egypt. Due to their unbelief, they roamed the desert until that generation of faithless people perished.

In contrast to those feeble-minded spies, there arose in Israel a giant of faith through whom God achieved so much for the people. This man was no other person than David, who later became the king of Israel. David rose to fame by killing an enemy warrior belonging to the nation of Philistia. Before this chance encounter, he had been anointed as king to succeed Saul who was on the throne at the time.

Whilst David was at the camp of the army, a warrior arose from the ranks of the Philistines and challenged Israel to a duel. This veteran warrior laid down the conditions for the duel, including making the people of the winner of the encounter victors. David was enraged at the insults that this warrior was hurling at Israel. So, though a mere youth, he volunteered to take on the champion. King Saul, who was initially doubtful of David's abilities, became even more skeptical when he could not wear the military uniform assigned to him. David went to war and prevailed, armed with his faith in God and a belief in his abilities. He won the war against the giant because of his positive confessions, which intimidated his opponent.

Notice that both the spies and David were confronted with giants whom they needed to remove. Whilst the spies recoiled into their shells and suffered death, David, by his act of bold faith, liberated an entire community. David blossomed because he had faith, but the spies perished because they had none. Learn from these examples. When in trouble, instead of fear, exercise faith so that you will be delivered. Let them serve as examples for you to make faith a hallmark of your life so that you will blossom.

THE NEXT LEVEL

When you optimize your faith, you will more than blossom; it will take you to the next level in your life. It will entrust you with opportunities you never thought possible before. It will lead you to distant lands; to places you never fathomed. Inversely, if you fail to exercise faith, it will condemn you to the bottom rungs of life.

In the *Inferno*, Dante Alighieri wrote: "Do not be afraid; our fate cannot be taken from us; it is a gift." This statement could only be true if the impact of faith is taken out of the equation. Each one of us, indeed, has a fate or a blueprint. However, if you fail to exercise faith your blueprint cannot be realized to its fullest. Conversely, if you constantly act in faith, your destiny will be shaped and enhanced in ways you never thought possible. It will open new horizons for you to see things only seen through the eyes of faith. It will show you how you can constantly energize your life and become unflappable.

The doors that faith will open for you are limitless. So, continue to yearn for greater faith. Do not be content with the level you have attained because there is always the possibility of moving higher and higher in faith and achieving more than you have already achieved.

Therefore, cherish your faith not only for the joy it brings you but for what it can lead you to accomplish for the common good of humanity. However, when your faith has taken you to those previously unperceived heights, be happy with your new image. At the same time, you should avoid the danger of taking a demeaning posture toward people who seem to have squandered all the growth opportunities that they had. Be confident but gracious where you are, but don't let that confidence reduce you to an arrogant and pretentious personality.

As you continue to build your faith, there are others whom you will meet who will think you are silly. However, do not get discouraged; continue to build your faith by striving for that which might be ridiculous to others but which you believe is true and achievable. Though they will think that you live in a world of absurdity and fantasy, be unfazed, nor use your faith to snare at them. Never let the unbelief and constant doubt of others derail your forward march. Continue to believe that your actions are for greater and better things. So, maintain faith in your abilities to get things done, and to take you to the next level.

OBSTACLES TO FAITH

We have seen the benefits we can accrue from optimizing our faith. I am sure it has drawn your attention to how important faith is for you to make inroads in your life. Nevertheless, several obstacles can stand in your way of exploiting your faith. You need to tackle these obstacles head-on because they can be the difference between failure and success. If you exercise them correctly, you will succeed, but if you don't, you will certainly fail.

The greatest obstacle to faith is unbelief. A lot of people harmlessly accept that they do not have faith. That confession becomes something that kills any desires they have to act in faith. When people confess to lacking faith, it is because they have little self-belief. They don't see themselves as capable, so they undermine their abilities to accomplish things.

Another enemy of faith is failure which can negatively affect your progress. However, do not allow the fear of failure to prevent you from ever taking a step of faith. When failure seems apparent, hold on and exercise patience so that you will not bow to its influence. Besides the fear of failure, fear of an uncertain future can also kill your faith. Fear allows you to see the obstacles but does not show you how to get over them. It puts stumbling blocks instead of providing steppingstones to step to higher ground.

Similarly, worry can choke your faith and leave you helplessly with unbelief and faithlessness. If you are a person who is always worried when it comes to taking any step, you will always remain in your position.

Additionally, do not seek rational explanations for any step you take in faith. You don't need to get an explanation for your faith. While you must see reason for anything that happens to you, you must not seek to assign reason to any occurrences. If you do that, you eliminate the supernatural.

The author Peter Borys wrote: "We must use our gift of reason to assist and predispose us for the development of pure faith that knows to a certainty beyond reason and sense."[27] Anytime you appeal to reason, you must use it to help unearth the different ways you can use your faith. Additionally, make it a vehicle for promoting your faith for greater achievements. Do not yield to any obstacles that will impede your faith. You were created in the image of God. Within you lies the power to be an overcomer. You can conquer the world with faith. Therefore, do not submit to the occasional blues; instead, let faith take over and thrust you in front.

---

27. Borys, Jr. Peter N. *Transforming Heart and Mind*. New York/Mahwah, N.J.: Paulist Press 2006, 140

CHAPTER ELEVEN
THERE IS HEALING IN FORGIVING

"Forgive, not because they deserve forgiveness, but because you deserve peace"
Author unknown

FORGIVENESS IS A HEALING BALM

Rachael had been suffering severe migraines for many years. This ailment had taken her to several doctors and specialists. However, despite all the doctoral visits, there was no cure. Since Rachael is a believer, she had also solicited prayers both from pastors and other believers. When I met her, she told me about her ordeal and how she had given up on seeking help for her situation. I encouraged her not to give up but to continue to seek help. Before we parted company, however, I counseled her to search for any element of unforgiveness or bitterness in her life.

Two weeks after our conversation, Rachael came back to see me. To my surprise, she told me the headaches were gone. Surprised, I asked her to tell me how a situation she had been dealing with for years could vanish in a blue moon. According to her, our conversation had garnered in her a desire to get to the root of her problem and to secure healing. During this time of self-examination, she remembered the resentment she had harbored against her stepmother.

She had blamed her parents' divorce on her and had hated her with a vengeance. Thus, at the time when she sat down to reexamine her life, she realized how that animosity for her stepmother still haunted her. When she came to that realization, she asked God to forgive her. After that, she paid a personal visit to her father and stepmother, whom she had not seen for several years. She asked them for forgiveness and also told them she no longer hated them for the development that somehow impacted her life.

After that visit, Rachael returned home, overwhelmed by the peace of God. Thereafter, she felt all the pain she was experiencing vanish. Rachael's experience clearly shows that unforgiveness can hurt a person. However, whenever we forgive, it orchestrates a healing process. This underscores how important forgiveness can be. When it is implemented, forgiveness is geared toward two main goals: to restore the relationships of humans with God and one person to another.

THE TWO-FOLD RESTORATIVE FUNCTION OF FORGIVENESS

Alan Paton, a South African novelist, once said; "When a deep injury is done us, we never recover until we forgive." Paton's observation underlies the restorative importance of forgiveness. It has two main functions. It is restorative for human-to-God and human-to-human relations. The Lord's Prayer typifies this relationship. That prayer teaches that humans become the benefactors of the goodwill of God when we forgive others who wrong us. On the human level, it is a healing balm both for the soul and the body.

Whenever a person learns to forgive, all the bitterness and hatred evaporates, and, in its place, the ability to nurture healthy relationships springs up. When we forgive others who offend us, it frees them to operate without guilt. At the same time, on a personal level, it helps us scale many obstacles. Similarly, the peace with God that forgiveness fosters sets a multiple of processes in place, cementing relationships on the human-to-human level.

FORGIVENESS RESTORES BROKEN RELATIONSHIPS

At the human-to-human level, the most notable benefit of forgiveness is the promotion of healthy relationships, because it papers over transgressions and cancels fault finding. The key relationships that forgiveness impacts are marriage, sibling, and sometimes communal relations.

Forgiveness is necessary because as easy as it might be to make new friends, it takes some work to keep them. If you are somebody who finds it hard to forgive, you cannot maintain any meaningful relationships.

Whenever someone wrongs you, it brings a gulf between the two of you. This divide deepens with time unless the two of you are resolved to patch up your differences. This applies equally to casual friendships and deeper relationships between parents and children and between spouses.

Such altercations usually result in rifts which have dire consequences. If it is between siblings, it results in acrimony, which should ordinarily not occur between blood relatives. If it is between spouses, it brings spite which can tear families apart. Divorce has become rampant in our world today because couples are unwilling to let go of their grievances and instead bear grudges against one another.

To forgive is one thing, and to forget is another. Often, even after you have forgiven an offense, it keeps haunting you. Though you may not necessarily forget the offense, do not let it continue to have a stranglehold on you. Because that situation will cripple you and render your forgiveness of no effect.

When you forgive others it not only frees them of the burden of guilt, but it also lightens any load you were carrying yourself. Furthermore, you create an atmosphere where friendships and relationships can be nurtured. The best example of how forgiveness can impact sibling relations is in the biblical story of Esau and Jacob. Esau was the elder of the two.

In the ancient Near East, the eldest son received his father's blessing and estate. However, Jacob, being craftier, exploited his brother to his advantage and managed to trick his father into blessing him. Seeping with anger, Esau sought to kill his brother, Jacob, so he ran to Mesopotamia. Whilst there, he amassed great wealth and a big family. Soon it was time to return home, but the threat of Esau loomed large.

Therefore, when he was returning and heard that his brother was coming to meet him, he became sorely afraid. However, his brother Esau had overcome his anger and saw no need to be bitter. Though Jacob wanted to appease his brother with cattle and sheep he was not prepared to receive them as he thought there was no need for appeasement. This move from Esau brought peace between the two siblings.

At the national or communal level, forgiveness can achieve a similar purpose. This is illustrated by the life of the anti-apartheid campaigner and former President of South Africa, Nelson Mandela. He was somebody who understood the language of forgiveness and its liberating effect. He was seen as a controversial figure by his detractors, who denounced him as a communist and terrorist.

Based on this assumption, he was censured and later imprisoned by the South African apartheid regime. Though as a black person living in a segregated South Africa, Mandela was more privileged than most black South Africans, he managed to get a good education. Nevertheless, he was deprived of some of the necessities of life.

Seeing the oppression of his people, he dedicated his life to fighting for their cause. For some time, he evaded capture even though he was sought by the apartheid police. Using forged documents, he was able to travel to champion the cause of the black South Africans. When finally, he was arrested, he was put on trial for different offenses at different times. Eventually, he was imprisoned along with six of his colleagues in a lonely prison, Robben Island. After serving 27 years of a life sentence, he was released.

Meanwhile, when in prison, both his mother and eldest son died, but he was not allowed to attend their funerals. After his release from prison, Mandela was soon to head the first black majority government in South Africa. Now the prisoner was the master of those who imprisoned him.

Two actions that Mandela took portrayed him as a giant among his peers. Upon assuming the presidency, he promised that he would step down after a single four-year term. He also promised not to take vengeance into his own hands. He formed a truth and reconciliation council to try to mend the relationship between all races, between the victim and the victimized.

These actions of Mandela not only united a nation but also cemented his legacy in the consciousness of the whole world. He was living proof of what happens to those who forgive. They become larger in the eyes of detractors as well as supporters. In the end, there were no critics or supporters, only enthusiasts.

FORGIVENESS RESTORES SELF-WORTH

The true intrinsic value of forgiveness is when individuals learn to forgive themselves. There are countless examples of people who learn to forgive themselves and reap manifold benefits.

The first example is from the biblical character Peter, one of the disciples of Jesus. Peter had promised to stay by the side of Jesus during his trial before the Jewish Supreme Court, the Sanhedrin. Nevertheless, when he beheld the cruelty displayed by the prosecution, Peter, fearing for his life, denied any knowledge of Jesus so that he would not suffer a similar fate.

This action demonstrably damaged Peter, who until then had been a trusted companion and the assumed leader to carry on Jesus' legacy. His denial, therefore, was seismic and mindboggling, especially for the fate of Jesus' bequest.

However, when after the resurrection of Jesus, Peter confessed his unfaithfulness, Jesus forgave him. After this encounter, Peter forgave himself and accepted the restoration which the Lord offered. Due to this all-important step Peter took, he not only agreed to lead the group but also acquired the power to focus on the ministry given to him instead of looking out for his parochial interests.

This example shows that if you can overcome the effects of any mistreatment meted out to you, you will regain your self-worth and be reenergized to continue with the business of life. Many things result from unforgiveness that can change the way we see ourselves. These include attacks on our personalities, and unkind words from parents, teachers, or peers.

These often grossly leave emotional wounds which in later years come back to haunt us in our relationships. Moreover, they destroy our self-confidence and make us put low values on ourselves.

However, once you learn to forgive you acquire the confidence to tackle the many issues life will throw at you. You will then be able to throw overboard any distorted and false view of your worth and what is important to you, you will begin to fathom how necessary it is to let bygones be bygones. When you forgive you regain your self-worth because the act grants you healing from the wound of the earlier offense and gives you a genuine heart of mercy and gratitude.

FORGIVENESS RESTORES A HEALTHY SELF-IMAGE

Not only does forgiveness restore a person's self-worth, but it also restores a healthful self-image and enhances their appearance. Unforgiveness fills any person with bitterness and rancor. When you become bitter, it changes your demeanor, dims your talents, and makes you a difficult person to live with. Furthermore, it scars even the most beautiful person and make them appear unattractive and mean-spirited. Once a person develops that ugly attitude, it affects his or her relationship building. Their inability to get relationships to work stem from the fact they are haunted by previous experiences.

The aftermath is usually hatred and rancor that goes to work against their self-interest. Such feeling cuts into your core as a human being and contributes to making or unmaking you.

As humans, we are made in the image of the creator. That image surrounds us with such awe that creatures other than humans are always overwhelmed in our presence. Any person who has remnants of unforgiveness harbors dark emotions around them.

Those emotions eventually injure the culprit as well as their environment. Once that happens, it not only distorts the personality within, but it also destroys the aura around you and makes you look ordinary. When your personality is compromised, you affect your environment negatively and reflect an unhealthful image of yourself. This unhealthful attitude then drives people and things away from you. In its place, it brings enmity, poverty, and scarcity.

The role of forgiveness, therefore, is to restore the positive self-image the creator endowed you with. It makes you appear strong and mature because forgiveness covers weakness with strength and hatred with love. Mark Twain said, "Forgiveness is the fragrance that the violet sheds on the heel that has crushed it."

The maturity you gain through forgiveness makes you accept other people as they are. Likewise, it makes you recognize that people are different in their makeup. Therefore, you learn to tolerate others for their weakness as well as their differences. The positive self-image that you gain makes you strong enough to stand against betrayal as well as rejection. Moreover, if you are a leader, you gain the strength to stand against rebellion from mentees and detractors alike.

When you nurture the spirit of forgiveness, the positive self-image that you regain gives you the ability to break new ground. It helps you to reap abundance instead of scarcity. It gives you a friendly and inviting demeanor, creates a healthful environment, and directs good things your way. and sets you on the path to greatness.

WHY FORGIVENESS IS NECESSARY

Whenever we forgive our detractors, it is not because they deserve it. Rather we forgive them so that we will not be enslaved by hatred and revulsion. This course of action is necessary because it give us peace, restores self-esteem, and improve our standing with our peers.

I met Quincy in Aurora, Colorado, where I live, an affable and congenial person who was kind to everybody. When I told him about this book and the topic of forgiveness, he shared his personal experience involving his ex-spouse and boyhood friend. His story went to show how forgiveness was necessary. He is the most cynical skeptic I have met in my life.

Quincy and his childhood friend, Kevin, lived a few miles apart. They shared all their hopes and aspirations as well as their fears. Their relationship was so cordial that each took for granted what the other said or did.

Both Quincy and Kevin married their high school sweethearts. Unfortunately, Kevin's marriage did not work out. The divorce took a toll on his desire to live, leading to homelessness. Quincy saw the plight of his friend and invited him into his matrimonial home. Kevin, however, abused Quincy's hospitality by engaging in adulterous relationships with his wife. Whilst the infidelity brought an end to Quincy's marriage the pain knew no end. He has never figured out how to forgive his estranged wife and former best friend.

Thus, his experience has left him bitter and disgruntled. He looks with distrust at any person who wants to draw closer. His attitude has not only prevented him from cultivating any meaningful relationships, but it has also kept him constantly depressed and cynical.

Such becomes the fate of any person who goes through an experience similar to Quincy's. Whenever one experiences painful and distasteful ordeals its effects may linger on. These unpleasant experiences make forgiveness very necessary. The reason is that, when you harbor resentment in your heart, it makes you feel undercut and mistreated. This kind of feeling will sap any appetite you have to continue living.

It is also necessary because as humans, we are equally capable of good and evil. Hence, developing the ability to forgive even implausible transgressions will help you cultivate love for other people. Likewise, forgiving others will help you get a grip on what you want to be as a person. If you learn to forgive, it helps you embrace the truth about yourself.

Moreover, it helps you break the cycle of passing blame for your shortcomings because of a constant lingering on others' wrongdoings. These steps will not only lift you out of the bottom rungs of society but will thrust you on an upward trajectory.

CHAPTER TWELVE

THE SECRETS OF SUPERSTARS

"Step up in front, head towards the sun, keep facing it and the dark shadows will not cross your path."
Claude M. Bristol

YOU CAN GET YOUR LIFE ON TRACK

One day, in my native country, Ghana, I was traveling to a village, and I had to cross a river to get there. At the bank of the river, there were several canoes but no one to ferry me across. I yelled out for somebody to help me, but there was no answer. Since it was almost night-time, I decided to ferry myself across before dusk came. Two things were working against me on that day: the crossing was near the confluence of a bigger river, and not only had I never paddled a canoe before, but I also did not know how to swim.

The first few minutes went all right. However, as I paddled downstream and saw the bigger river, I was gripped with fear. Just then, my canoe started to drift towards the big river. I realized I had a decision to make. I could give in to crippling fear, capsize, and get drowned, or I could muster up courage and paddle to shore.

Similarly, we each can make the hard decisions that get our lives on track or give up and wallow in oblivion. Let me reassure you that if there is breath in you, you have not lost the fight to salvage your life. It is unfortunate that earlier in your life, you might have messed up, or you might not even have started to live.

Notwithstanding, it is not the time to give up but a time to give yourself a fresh start. Strive to take hold of what life has to offer to become the person God made you to be, a superstar.

David Schwartz has categorized people into three groups: the homeless who live on skid row, the ordinary people who live in the mediocrity lane, and the highly effective people who live in the land of success. In his opinion, those who live on skid row encountered problems and yielded to defeat; those who live in mediocrity have accepted their state in life; while those who are successful are always striving to do more.

At this point, your task is not to be hard on yourself for past mistakes. Instead, what you should do is to up the ante. Ask yourself how you can do better; and how you can improve on your earlier performances.

If one door is closed, another will open. Therefore, do not worry about what you missed; think about what is available and what is upcoming. Stop thinking about what you failed to do; think about what you can do now. Don't think about what could have been. Consider the many possibilities that are open to you now.

The idea of thinking about what could have been will, at best, only make you unhappy if you are not miserable already. Take hold of life and let it be your crown and glory. Do not be among the multitude who have already given up. Do not continue to sit down while all the goodness of the creator passes you by.

Today our world is better off because some people overcame their fears and shortfalls and became trailblazers in their chosen professions. You also, by tapping into your God-given talents, can help find solutions for people to deal with the day-to-day changes in life.

YOU CAN STILL BE AT YOUR OPTIMAL BEST

Undeniably, every human being has a spark within. Nevertheless, we often put the brakes on what we can do by assuming that we might not be like some others who are especially gifted. Such a mindset largely prevents us from realizing our true potential.

These limitations we put on ourselves do not only shackle us, but they also prevent us from hearing our inner voice of wisdom. Moreover, our limiting thoughts tend to control our ability to see the world more productively. Often, the limitations we put on ourselves continually plague us with negativism. That tendency often saddles us with a narrow view of the world such that we do not see anything good in others, let alone in our own lives.

At this juncture, I want you to critically examine your life. Perhaps it will help you gain an understanding of why you may be seeing the world in an underwhelming sense instead of in a more fruitful way.

That scrutiny will also give you further insight into the succession of letdowns, disappointments, and frustrations that seem to bedevil your life and want to sap any happiness that you are supposed to experience. Know that the end of the road for such unfulfilled needs may lead you into depression or even the possibility of taking your own life. However, things need not deteriorate to that extent. The reason is that there are viable steps you can take to reignite the spark within and become your optimal best.

CHANGE YOUR BELIEF SYSTEM

The first of the steps you need to take to reach your optimal best is to change your belief system. Remember, many people walk haplessly through life because they often carry the wrong beliefs. Such people often look down on their own abilities because that is what they have been made to believe about themselves. They have been deceived into believing they are nothing. Therefore, they continue to put low premiums on themselves.

If you have bought into such a false narrative, you will have to change your way of thinking to help you derive maximum benefit from your talents. To engender this change, you should ignite your inner power to resurrect your sleeping giant. When you can correct this flawed thinking, it will open your eyes to see the talents you have. To discover what your talent is, you should begin to do the things you know best. Arrest any tendency to move from project to project because it will slow down the true unearthing of your talent.

As Albert Winseman et al assert: "There is something about the concept of talents and strengths that just "feels right." When we discover our talents, when we give them a name, something resonates deep within us."[28] So look for what you can do best and work hard at it. Polish it so that you will be of use to yourself and the society you live in.

You must have a driving force to recapture your inner glow. This quest should begin with your desire to live in the present. So, forget the past with its failures and live in the now so that you can prepare well for the future, which lies wide ahead with prospects.

When you change your belief system, it will also help you change the way you see others. You will no longer be critical of others. Instead, you will learn to trust people more. This attitude change will surely change the way others perceive you. They will see you as a reasonable person who is more accommodating and amenable to change. There is an added advantage in changing your belief system. Since your world is no longer that of scarcity and need, you will begin to see abundance in your life. That, in turn, will give you the strength to always go in for more.

BE A PERSON OF FAITH

The next step vital for changing your fortunes is to become a person of faith. I am sure you might have heard the saying, "Walk by faith and not by sight." Life is not all that we see. The major part remains largely unseen. It is those who have faith and are willing to leap into the world of the unknown

---

28 . Winseman, Albert L., Donald O. Clifton & Curt Liesveld. *Living Your Strengths: Discover your God-given talents and inspire your community.* New York: Gallup Press, 2003-2004, 8.

who achieve the unachievable. You, therefore, should develop your faith to believe in things yet unseen.

It is good to be pragmatic about your beliefs. Nevertheless, that should not preclude you from believing in things you do not yet see. Challenge your belief system to see if it can guarantee you success in your new quest for upward mobility. Assume a stance that will be able to ensure that you are always prime for bigger and greater things in your life.

Furthermore, it will be good to build on your faith by inculcating a habit of constantly praying and bringing your needs before God. The reason is that, in prayer you express your sole dependence on God and his ability to not only right things in your life, but to be able to help you maintain your newly found desire to succeed.

Use faith to build your self-confidence so that you can begin to take on tasks you shunned before. Believe that you can do all things through Christ, who gives you strength. Find suitable words you can use to motivate yourself. Write those words on a piece of cardboard paper and put it by the mantel of your bed. Affirm it every day when you are going to bed and first thing when you wake up from bed. Use this power of suggestions to lift you up from the doldrums.

Above all, see the connection between prayer and faith. When you pray for anything, believe that you have it. Do not give room to any ounce of doubt. Always assail doubt with faith and see if you will not be a winner.

Likewise, use Laura Fortgang's "why-what" approach, mentioned in chapter one, in your quest for answers. Stop asking why you are not making it in life, and rather ask what you can do to change the situation you find yourself in. Stop musing over the past and begin to do and believe in what you can be. Do not allow discontent in your life to prevent you from making the strides you are to make in life.

Tackle any inability to make firm decisions headlong. Decide on one thing, and do not change your mind. If you continue to do this, with time, you will forget that you were that indecisive person. Is your problem a lack of motivation in life or a willingness to easily give up when the going becomes tough? Well, don't give up because you have Christ to help you.

Have you been facing adversity? Well, do not fold up because you have an advocate, the Lord Jesus Christ, who intercedes and pleads on your behalf every day. If you do not crumble and fold up in the face of adversity, you are sure able to make it through the next step. Believe that your road to recovery begins with your recognition that you need change.

CHANGE YOURSELF, CHANGE YOUR CIRCUMSTANCES

Things are surely set in their ways. For example, the tidal waves will always alternate between high and low, they will never change. The earth will always revolve around the sun, it will never change. Tough times will always be there, and so will joblessness. Some people will always be rich, and others will always be poor. This suggests that the circumstances of our world will never change. You will always have to go to the shop, and prices will always go up. Nevertheless, the fact that things are set in their ways does not mean all is hopeless.

There is always a glimmer of hope because there is one thing that can change, YOU. If you change yourself, your circumstances will change. To become superstars, we each need to change something in our lives. That desire for change can help you experience an uplift. When you are denied a position, do not blame others but yourself. Perhaps your attitude drives away people who should support you.

When you have no friends, do not blame others for not being magnanimous. Perhaps, you do not take the initiative to make friends. Remember, we all reap what we sow. If you smile at people, they will smile back. If you care for others, they will care for you in return.

Learn to live life to the fullest so that you will attain your set objectives. Your pathway to achievement lies in your ability to recognize what you want to be. Focus on the goals you have set for your life and work for their attainment. Whilst at this, constantly work to improve yourself. The key to success lies in self-improvement. Change the way you talk to people. Show genuine affection to those you interact with. Firm your handshakes, smile more often, and let others feel welcome in your presence. In short, change your attitude so that you will gain the recognition that you need to break down any barriers in your life.

FORGIVE, MUSTER COURAGE, AND MARCH ON

Certainly, carrying out the preceding suggestions is essential. However, you have to crown all your efforts with forgiveness. Never underestimate what forgiveness can accomplish. It is essential because it can act as a channel to lead you to greater heights that hitherto have remained hidden from you. Hence, forgive others who may have wronged you, but above all else, forgive yourself.

Everybody goes through life making mistakes. Even from this day onwards, you will still make mistakes, so forgive yourself so that you can move on. What you need to do is to learn to constantly forgive yourself and muster the courage to deal with life's many problems. In the past, you may not have been able to nail down a sustainable job because of erroneously believing that you had no talent. There is good news for you. Everybody has talent, and this means you possess some talent, too.

Take a positive approach to life generally. Let everything you do scream courage and confidence. Confidence begins with posture and the way you carry yourself. Walk chest out. Think tall and talk tall. Don't make too many concessions in your speech. Do not mumble in your speech but speak clearly and to the point always. Be assertive without being rude.

Try to complete your sentences as often as you can. If you do not complete your sentences, people lose interest in what you have to say. Likewise, stop apologizing and making excuses for yourself. Know that the knack to apologize for any little thing will portray you as a person lacking in confidence and having low self-esteem. Recognize that in this life, it is not only you who makes mistakes.

Everyone makes mistakes, plenty of them. Those who have been able to overcome the blues of what their mistakes thrust on them are those people who have been able to turn their weaknesses into strengths.

Above all, be mindful of how you live your life as the Bible urges, "Look carefully then how you walk, not as unwise but as wise, making the best use of the time, because the days are evil. Therefore do not be foolish, but understand what the will of the Lord is" (Ephesians 5:15-17).

Let the work of Christ be manifested in your life. Believe that; "if anyone is in Christ, he is a new creation. The old has passed away; behold, the new has come" (2 Corinthians 5:17). Which part of "new" is hard to comprehend? If you entrusted your life to Christ, you are new, period.

Your old life of failure and underachievement is gone. So is your life of pessimism and faithlessness. Let this renewed nature take possession of your thinking and, in fact, all aspects of your life. Once you have assumed your new nature, it will thrust on you a renewed hope to strive for those things that will give meaning to your life.

You may agree with me that in life, there are valleys and hills, joy and sadness. Problems will not cease in this world. Therefore, begin your day everyday by pumping up yourself with an infectious dose of optimism. Don't let a day go by without re-affirming your strengths over weaknesses.

Instead of giving in to negativity, embrace optimism. Rather than acceding to mediocrity, strive for excellence. Make this infectious mood of optimism permanent and commonplace in your life, and it will wipe out the sadness and misfortunes that are associated with life. These are the secrets that top-notch people know, and now you also know.

BIBLIOGRAPHY

Allyn, David. *I Can't Believe I Just Did That: How (Seemingly) Small Embarrassments Can Wreak Havoc in Your Life—and What You Can Do to Put a Stop to Them.* New York: Penguin Group Inc., 2004.

Asmis, Elizabeth. *Epicureanism*, In Anchor Bible Dictionary Vol. 2, David Noel Freedman Editor-in-Chief, [Toronto: Doubleday Publishers], 559-561, 1992.

Baldwin, Charles Sears. Ancient Rhetoric and Poetic: Interpreted from Representative Works. Gloucester, Mass.: Peter Smith, 1959.

Borys, Jr. Peter N. *Transforming Heart and Mind.* New York/Mahwah, N.J.: Paulist Press 2006.

Bristol, Claude M. *The Magic of Believing* (Audio Book). Narrated by Mitch Horowtz

Clark, Donald Lemen. Rhetoric in Greco-Roman Education. Morningside Heights, New York: Columbia University Press, 1957.

Clarke, M. L. Rhetoric at Rome: A Historical Survey. London: Cohen and West, 1968.

Copeland, Gloria. *God's Master Plan for Your Life: Ten Keys to Fulfilling Your Destiny.* New York: G. P. Putman's Sons, 2008.

Copeland, Rita. Rhetoric, hermeneutics, and translation in the Middle Ages: Academic Traditions and Vernacular Texts. Cambridge, England: Cambridge University Press, 1991.

Dyer, Wayne W. *The Power of Intention: Learning to Co-create Your World Your Way.* Carlsbad, California: Hay House Inc., 2004.

------------- *I Can See Clearly Now.* Carlsbad, California: Hay House Inc., 2014

Edward Jr., O. C. A History of Preaching Nashville: Abingdon Press, 2004.

Engberg-Pedersen, Troels ed. Paul Beyond the Judaism/Hellenism Divide. Louisville, London and Leiden: Westminster John Knox Press, 2001.

Fortgang, Laura Berman. *Living Your Best Life: Ten Strategies for Getting from Where You Are to Where You're Meant to Be.* New York: Jeremy P. Tarcher/Putman, 2001

Grant, Robert M. First and Second Clement Vol. 2 of the Apostolic Fathers: A New Translation and Commentary. New York: Thomas Nelson, 1965.

Hall, Robert G. "Arguing Like an Apocalypse: Galatians and Ancient Topos Outside the Greco-Roman Rhetorical Tradition." New Testament Studies 42.3 (1996) 434-453

Herford, R. Travers. Judaism in the New Testament Period. London: The Lindsey Press, 1928.

Hewitt, Les & Charlie Self. *The Power of Faithful Focus: A Practical Christian Guide to Spiritual & Personal Abundance.* Deerfield Beach Florida: Faith Communication, Inc. 2004.

James, William. *The Will to Believe and Other Essays in Popular Philosophy* [New York: Dover Publications, Inc. 1956

————————— The Essential Writings. Edited by Bruce W. Wilshire, New York: Harper and Row 1971.

William James: in the maelstrom of American modernism, a biography, by Robert D. Richardson. Houghton Mifflin Company. Boston/New York 2006.

James William: Selected Writings Introduction by Robert Coles. New York: Book-of the-month Club 1997

James, William. The Varieties of Religious Experience: A Study in human nature. Foreword 1958 by the New American Library of world literature, Inc.

Jeremy Carrette Ed. William James and the varieties of religious experience

Johnson. Luke Timothy. Religious Experience in Earliest Christianity: A Missing Dimension In New Testament Studies. Minneapolis, Minn.: Fortress Press, 1998.

Kennedy, George A. A New History of Classical Rhetoric. Princeton: Princeton University Press 1994.

————————— The Art of Rhetoric in the Roman World Princeton, N.J.: Princeton University Press, 1972.

————————— The Art of Persuasion in Greece. Princeton, N.J.: Princeton University Press, 1963.

————————— Aristotle.On rhetoric: a theory of civic discourse; newly translated, with introduction, notes, and appendixes by George A. Kennedy. New York: Oxford University Press, 1991.

————————— Classical Rhetoric and its Christian and Secular Tradition from Ancient to Modern Times. Chapel Hill: University of North Carolina 1980.

------------- *Quintilian*. New York: Twayne Publishers, Inc. 1969.

------------- New Testament Interpretation through Rhetorical Criticism. Chapel Hill: University of North Carolina Press, 1994.

Mitchell, Margaret M. Paul and the Rhetoric of Reconciliation: An Exegetical Investigation of the Language and Composition of 1 Corinthians. Tübingen: J.C.B. Mohr (P. Siebeck), 1991.

Moore, George Foot. Judaism in the First Centuries of the Christian Era: The Age of the Tannaim. New York: Schocken Books, 1971.

Murphy, James Jerome. Aristotle's Rhetoric in the Middle Ages. Chicago: National Assoc. of Teachers of Speech, 1965.

------------- Latin rhetoric and education in the Middle Ages and Renaissance Aldershot, Hants, England; Burlinton, VT: Ashgate, 2005.

------------- Rhetoric in the Middle Ages: a history of rhetorical theory from Saint Augustine to the Renaissance. Berkeley: University of California Press, 1974.

Truth and convention in the Middle Ages: rhetoric, representation, and reality Cambridge; England; New York: Cambridge University Press, 1991.

Roberts W. Rhys and Ingram Bywater, Trans. The Rhetoric and the Poetics of Aristotle. Introduction by Edward P. J. Corbett, New York: The Modern Library 1954 & 1984.

Russell, Donald A. Greek Declamation. Cambridge: Cambridge University Press, 1982.

Kennedy, George A. Editor and Translator. Quintilian I: The Orator's Education Bk. 1-2 Cambridge, Massachusetts and London, England: Harvard University Press, 2001.

------------- Quintilian: The Orator's Education Books 3-5. Cambridge, Massachusetts and London England: Harvard University Press, 2001.

------------- Quintilian: The Orator's Education Books 9-10. Cambridge, Massachusetts and London England: Harvard University Press, 2001.

------------- Quintilian: The Orator's Education Books 11-12. Cambridge, Massachusetts and London England: Harvard University Press, 2001.

Rosenthal, Gilbert S. "Both These and Those" Pluralism within Judaism, In Conservative Judaism 56.3 (2004) 3-20.

Schemeller, Thomas. *Stoicism*, In Anchor Bible Dictionary Vol. 6, David Noel Freedman Editor-in-Chief, [Toronto: Doubleday Publishers], 210-214, 1992.

Schwartz, David J. The Magic of Thinking Big. Chatsworth California: Wilshere Book Co. 1959.

Todorov, Tzvetan. Theories of the Symbol, trans. Catherine Porter. Ithaca: Cornell University Press, 1982.

Tripolitis, Antonia. *Religion of the Hellenistic-Roman Age*. Grand Rapids, Michigan and Cambrigde, U. K.: William B. Eerdmans Publishing Company 2002.

Watson, Duane F. A Rhetorical Analysis of 2 John According to Greco-Roman Convention New Testament Studies 35.1 (1989) 104-130

------------- "James 2 In light of Greco-Roman Schemes of Argumentation." New Testament M Studies 39.1 (1993) 94-121

Watts, N.H. Cicero, the Speeches with an English Translation, London: William Heinemann; New York: G. P. Putnam's Sons, 1923.

Weiss, Douglas. *Get A Grip: How to Take Control of the Things that are Controlling You.* Lake Mary, Florida: Siloam A Strang Company, 2006.

Winseman, Albert L., Donald O. Clifton & Curt Liesveld. *Living Your Strengths: Discover your God-given talents and inspire your community.* New York: Gallup Press, 2003-2004.

Young, Ed. Outrageous, Contagious Joy: Five Big Questions to Help You Discover One Great Life. New York: The Berkley Publishing Group, 2007.

INTERNET SOURCES

The Story of the Piccolo Player<www.storiesforpreaching.com accessed August 12, 2015

Angelica Hopes quotes<goodreads.com/author/show/44911745.angelica_hopes accessed January 31, 2015

A Spirit Controlled Temperament Sermon Select< http://www.nelsonprice.com/a-spirit-controlled-temperament-2/ Accessed March 26, 2015

A Dr. D. W. Ekstrand Study On "The Four Human Temperaments" <http://www.thetransformedsoul.com/additional-studies/miscellaneous-studies/the-four-human-temperaments accessed March 26, 2015

Jackie Robinson at Baseball Hall of Fame<http://baseballhall.org/hof/robinson-jackie accessed September 13, 2015

Biography of Jackie Robinson<http://www.biography.com/people/jackie-robinson-9460813 accessed September 13, 2015

Wikipedia on Jackie Robinson<http://en.wikipedia.org/wiki/Jackie Robinson accessed September 13, 2015

BIBLIOGRAPHY

http://listverse.com/2013/12/24/10-refreshing-stories-rich-people-who-gave-their-fortunes-away/accessed September 20, 2015

A comparison of river salinity to ocean salinity <http://omp.gso.uri.edu/ompweb/doee/science/physical/chsal1.htm accessed September 29, 2015

Life is too short to Worry <http://www.lifehack.org/articles/communication/20-things-life-too-short-worry-about.html accessed September 29, 2015

The 5_Step Model for stopping Worry<http://psychcentral.com/lib/5-steps-to-reduce-worrying-and-anxiety/accessed September 29, 2015

The Four Personalities<blog.Bretthard. in accessed March 4, 2020.

ABOUT THE AUTHOR

Pastor and teacher **Akwasi Oppong Ofori** is an ordained minister of the Ghana Baptist Convention. Formerly the Lead Pastor at Solid Rock Baptist Church in Aurora, Colorado, he also served as the first chairperson of the North American Baptist Association of the Ghana Baptist Convention. He is the author of two other books, *Recovering Storytelling for Ghanaian Preaching*, and *I Will Lift Up My Cup*. Originally trained as a teacher at the Wesley College of Education in Kumasi Ghana, he has a Diploma in Biblical Studies and a Bachelor of Theology (BTh) degrees from the Christian Service University College in Kumasi Ghana and the International Baptist Theological Seminary in Prague the Czech Republic respectively. Rev. Ofori also holds a Master of Divinity (M. Div.) from Denver Seminary in Colorado, USA, and a Master of theology (Th.M.) from the Toronto School of Theology of the University of Toronto Canada. Rev. Ofori is completed by his wife and two surviving children.

www.ingramcontent.com/pod-product-compliance
Lightning Source LLC
Chambersburg PA
CBHW020333010526
44119CB00002B/50